RAND NATIONAL DEFENSE RESEARCH INSTITUTE

T0269994

Defense Institution Building in Africa

An Assessment

Michael J. McNerney, Stuart E. Johnson, Stephanie Pezard,
David Stebbins, Renanah Miles, Angela O'Mahony, Chaoling Feng,
Tim Oliver

Prepared for the Office of the Secretary of Defense
Approved for public release; distribution unlimited

For more information on this publication, visit www.rand.org/t/RR1232

Library of Congress Cataloging-in-Publication Data is available for this publication.
ISBN: 978-0-8330-9240-3

Published by the RAND Corporation, Santa Monica, Calif.
© Copyright 2016 RAND Corporation
RAND® is a registered trademark.

Cover: U.S. Air Force photo by Staff Sgt. Christopher Ruano.

Limited Print and Electronic Distribution Rights

This document and trademark(s) contained herein are protected by law. This representation of RAND intellectual property is provided for noncommercial use only. Unauthorized posting of this publication online is prohibited. Permission is given to duplicate this document for personal use only, as long as it is unaltered and complete. Permission is required from RAND to reproduce, or reuse in another form, any of its research documents for commercial use. For information on reprint and linking permissions, please visit www.rand.org/pubs/permissions.html.

The RAND Corporation is a research organization that develops solutions to public policy challenges to help make communities throughout the world safer and more secure, healthier and more prosperous. RAND is nonprofit, nonpartisan, and committed to the public interest.

RAND's publications do not necessarily reflect the opinions of its research clients and sponsors.

Support RAND
Make a tax-deductible charitable contribution at
www.rand.org/giving/contribute

www.rand.org

Preface

Many African governments are beset with challenges stemming from fragile security environments and governance institutions. The U.S. Department of Defense identifies building strong defense institutions as a priority for the region. Defense institution building (DIB) includes activities that promote effective, accountable, transparent, and responsive defense institutions. This report assesses U.S. DIB efforts in Africa and provides insights on possible improvements to planning and execution.

This research was sponsored by the U.S. Department of Defense and conducted within the International Security and Defense Policy Center of the RAND National Defense Research Institute, a federally funded research and development center sponsored by the Office of the Secretary of Defense, the Joint Staff, the Unified Combatant Commands, the Navy, the Marine Corps, the defense agencies, and the defense Intelligence Community.

For more information on the RAND International Security and Defense Policy Center, see www.rand.org/nsrd/ndri/centers/isdp or contact the director (contact information is provided on the web page).

Contents

Figures and Tables

Figures

Tables

Summary

Defense institutions play a critical role sustaining military forces and ensuring that those forces are accountable to and supportive of civilian institutions. Any country can find sustaining such institutions a challenge, but the challenge is particularly acute for many African nations, where democratic governance, economic and social well-being, and security, as well as the resources to address these issues, can be limited or simply not exist. Such challenges notwithstanding, the 2014 Quadrennial Defense Review noted that, in Africa, "there is also significant opportunity to develop stronger governance institutions and to help build professional, capable military forces that can partner with the United States to address the full spectrum of regional security challenges."[1]

This report assesses U.S. efforts in defense institution building (DIB) in Africa and suggests possible improvements to planning and execution. It first defines DIB and reviews some best practices from DIB and security sector reform (SSR) experiences. It also highlights how DIB activities serve U.S. official strategic guidance for Africa. The report then examines how DIB is currently planned and executed in Africa and describes the range of programs that are available to U.S. planners for that purpose. It also provides a structured approach to aid in the prioritization of such programs. The report then analyzes DIB efforts in two African nations—Liberia and Libya. Finally, it examines how other institutions and countries undertake DIB by taking a

---

[1] U.S. Department of Defense (DoD), *Quadrennial Defense Review 2014*, Washington, D.C., 2014, p. 5.

closer look at the DIB activities of DoD's regional centers, as well as the relatively extensive experience of two key U.S. allies—the United Kingdom and France—in this domain.

What Is DIB and Why Is It Relevant for Africa?

DIB aims to promote effective, transparent, and responsive institutions in a variety of ways. Its goals include improving civilian control of the military, building respect for the rule of law, and improving military professionalism. What it does *not* do is focus on the operational readiness or tactical capabilities of the host nation's military.

A number of U.S. organizations engage in DIB activities, most notably DoD and the State Department. DoD is a major DIB provider through programs that include (but are not limited to) the Defense Institutional Reform Initiative (DIRI), the Defense Institute of International Legal Studies (DIILS), the Ministry of Defense Advisors Program (MoDA), and the regional centers for security studies. Since DIB also aims at professionalizing defense personnel, any institution that engages in professional military education (PME)—as long as the students are officers or in a managerial position—is also part of the overall DIB enterprise. Because of its oversight of several other DIB programs and—more importantly—U.S. foreign policy, the State Department is a full partner in DIB oversight and implementation.

Numerous countries on the African continent can benefit from DIB. The challenges facing African militaries include a lack of military professionalism; a high incidence of mutinies; human rights violations; and complicity in such illegal activities as wildlife trafficking, politicization of the defense apparatus, and collusion with economic actors.[2] Some countries have undergone large-scale reforms of their institutions, such as Liberia and Sierra Leone after their civil wars. Others—

---

[2] See Emile Ouédraogo, *Advancing Military Professionalism in Africa*, Washington D.C.: Africa Center for Strategic Studies, Research Paper No. 6, July 2014, pp. 3, 4, 11, and 18–20; and Herbert M. Howe, *Ambiguous Order: Military Forces in African States*, Lynne Rienner Publishers, 2001.

for example, Mali—are seeing a transition from operationally focused assistance activities to institutionally focused activities.

Lessons for DIB from Security Sector Reform History

Three types of DIB stand out from SSR practice. First, DIB can be accomplished through large-scale, sweeping reforms that overhaul defense establishments and replace them with more efficient and accountable ones. Second, advisors can be sent to provide support to key defense officials in the partner nation. Finally, DIB can involve educating or training the personnel who will fill key positions in the defense institutions of the partner nation.

Because DIB is the part of SSR that targets defense institutions, it can benefit from some of the lessons and best practices that have been developed for SSR. Such lessons include the need to tailor SSR and DIB to the specific conditions of the partner; the difficulty of conducting discrete interventions, since all institutions interact and, to a certain extent, rely on each other; and the positive effect of the following factors on SSR and DIB's chances of success: commitment of the leadership, ensuring that new institutions reflect the country's history and culture, and fostering consultations within the government and between the government and civil society.[3]

We found little evidence, however, that these lessons were being systematically documented to support DIB planners and implementers. As discussed in the report, written guidance and other documents that help stakeholders truly understand DIB (as well as SSR) and implement it effectively is limited.

Even more challenging than understanding SSR principles and DIB best practices—many of which are well-understood in the field— is improving the mechanics of how to make the U.S. bureaucracy function in a way that implements DIB in accordance with those principles and best practices. There are significant structural constraints

---

[3] Nicole Ball, "Reforming Security Sector Governance," *Conflict, Security & Development*, Vol. 4, No. 3, 2004, pp. 510–511.

that inhibit robust and effective DIB. For example, the significant mismatch between the resources required and those available (including outside DoD) prevents the United States from implementing SSR and DIB within ideal parameters. There is also a mismatch between the long timelines required for SSR and DIB to take hold and the extremely short (usually one year) funding cycles of most U.S. programs. Finally, the stovepiped nature of congressional authorities makes it almost impossible to implement a comprehensive, whole-of-government approach. Because the scale of these challenges can seem overwhelming, this report focuses primarily on small, concrete steps DoD officials can implement relatively quickly and easily.

DIB's Contribution to U.S. Strategic Objectives for Africa

As part of our review of DIB, we analyzed over a dozen U.S. government strategic guidance documents and condensed 48 objectives into eight core objectives for Africa. We found that DIB contributes directly to supporting two U.S. core objectives for Africa: having African military forces that are capable, accountable, and professional; and ensuring that these forces are supported by effective, legitimate, and professional security institutions.

These two objectives, furthermore, directly affect several other core objectives. Effective security institutions, as well as professional and accountable military forces, provide the conditions that make it possible to deter extremism and combat transnational threats. DIB also creates a virtuous circle by reinforcing the country's ability to provide security to its citizens and the region as a whole. For instance, having legitimate and accountable security institutions reduces the risk of abuses against the civilian population and repression of ethnic and religious minorities, which can provide fertile ground for radicalization and extremism, whether homegrown or transnational. DIB also increases a partner nation's security—by reducing internal tensions—and legitimacy by providing security to its neighbors. In this way, DIB objectives can form useful "stepping stones" for other U.S. strategic objectives in Africa. Despite this, we found that the linkages between DIB objectives and other U.S. objectives were poorly understood.

Recommendations

Given the many lessons important to implementing DIB effectively in Africa and the importance of DIB for advancing U.S. objectives there, we offer the following recommendations:

- The Office of the Secretary of Defense (OSD) and U.S. Africa Command (AFRICOM) should jointly develop a DIB best practices briefing tailored to Africa for use by AFRICOM staff, U.S. embassy country team officials, and other stakeholders. This briefing could address strategic guidance—highlighting the central role of DIB in accomplishing U.S. defense objectives in Africa—as well as lessons from past institutional reform efforts.
- More broadly, we recommend that DoD leaders work with Congress to address the need for additional DIB-related resources (both for DoD and other agencies) and to facilitate whole-of-government, long-term DIB efforts.

From DIB Guidance to Execution: The Roles of OSD, AFRICOM, and African Partners

From guidance to execution, DIB presents specific challenges, particularly as it ties in to other security cooperation efforts. For example, many policymakers in OSD want a top-down approach to institution building. Such an approach is valuable because institutions are located at the headquarters level and closer to powerful decisionmakers, and because the best sources of talent for strengthening partner institutions are often current or former officials from institutions in the United States that have counterparts in the African nation. As a result, OSD may need to play a more active role in DIB planning compared with most other security cooperation programs, which are controlled to a greater degree by combatant commands.

Frequent misunderstandings between stakeholders represent another challenge. A more systematic and strategic dialogue is needed to improve understanding and buy-in from AFRICOM and U.S. embassy planners and other stakeholders. In addition, the Defense Security Cooperation Agency's (DSCA's) role is often misunderstood. Although DSCA plays a crucial role integrating thousands of security cooperation activities executed each year, its role in DIB specifically is unclear.

Communication issues also take place at the level of AFRICOM planners, who need clearly articulated requirements. Planning documents, along with stakeholder conferences, can be important coordination mechanisms, particularly for efforts like DIB that focus on the strategic level of cooperation and have many stakeholders within and outside DoD.

Finally, it is critical to understand the perspective of African partners. Helping a partner country reform its institutions can be a particularly sensitive topic, because these efforts can touch on issues of national sovereignty more than, say, training an army battalion. DIB implementers must have both relevant substantive expertise and strong relationship-building skills attuned to the region. Currently, those most responsible for engaging with partner officials appear to have insufficient preparation and guidance for explaining DIB opportunities to African officials and for tying DIB to other U.S. and African country goals.

Although some formal guidance exists and communication goes on, we found the guidance to be insufficient and communication to be ad hoc, given the complexity of DIB and how it relates to security cooperation more generally.

Recommendations

Given the particular challenges posed by planning and implementing DIB in the context of security cooperation, we recommend that

- OSD, DSCA, and AFRICOM develop a security cooperation playbook with a prominent section on DIB, written in simple language describing how DIB supports other U.S. objectives and how it can be used with African partners. The playbook would help planners and implementers coordinate activities and communicate with African partners.

- AFRICOM develop guidance for country desk officers to consistently coordinate DIB planning efforts across the command and country teams. This would help harmonize DIB-related objectives in country-level plans, such as AFRICOM's country cooperation plans and the State Department's integrated country strategies.

Given the challenges of both vertical (headquarters to field) and horizontal coordination, we also identified opportunities to strengthen coordination within the U.S. government. We recommend improvements to DoD organizational structures and relationships in three ways:

- AFRICOM should strengthen its DIB coordinator office and institutionalize an annual DIB conference (perhaps in concert with an annual security cooperation conference).
- DSCA should take full responsibility for DIB program management and play a greater role in integrating DIB with the full range of U.S. government security cooperation activities.
- OSD should set up a DIB enterprise liaison at AFRICOM as part of AFRICOM's DIB coordinator office. Ideally, this liaison could come from a central DIB enterprise organization that coordinates DIB across all of DoD and reports to DoD's DIB Coordination Board.[4]

---

[4] The DIB enterprise concept is described in Walter L. Perry, Stuart E. Johnson, Stephanie Pezard, Gillian S. Oak, David Stebbins, and Chaoling Feng, *Defense Institution Building: An Assessment*, Santa Monica, Calif.: RAND Corporation, RR-1176-OSD, forthcoming. The DIB Coordination Board will be established upon approval of DoD Directive 5205.JB, *Defense Institution Building* (Under Secretary of Defense for Policy, *Defense Institution Building (DIB)*, Draft Department of Defense Directive 5205.JB, Washington, D.C.: Department of Defense, as of May 11, 2015).

Identifying DIB Programs Relevant to Africa

Our review of security cooperation programs relevant to DIB in Africa found that there are more DIB-related programs than is generally thought. We identified 47 U.S. government programs that can be leveraged to address specific DIB requirements. DIB programs like MoDA and the Wales (formerly Warsaw) Initiative Fund have expanded their geographic reach, while relatively new programs like the Security Governance Initiative and the Africa Military Education Program are focused on Africa. While navigating such a large and varied array of programs can be challenging, they provide options for implementing DIB in ways that may be more palatable to sensitive partners—for example, offering an exchange of personnel to a partner nation reluctant to host a U.S. advisor. Thus, strengthening DIB efforts in Africa does not require creating new programs, but rather focusing existing programs in this direction. For example, the U.S. National Guard's State Partnership Program could increase the number of partnerships in Africa and focus engagements on DIB.

Finding the right mix of programs and integrating them into a comprehensive, sustainable DIB effort that also supports overall security cooperation goals requires extensive training. Despite some progress in this area, our analysis found that current training for DIB planners and implementers remains insufficient and somewhat ad hoc.

Recommendation

Given that U.S. officials are not sufficiently trained to effectively leverage the full array of security cooperation programs that can support DIB, we recommend that

- OSD, DSCA, and AFRICOM collaborate to institute improved DIB training through the inclusion of a DIB familiarization module in DSCA's Defense Institute of Security Assistance Management Course and by having AFRICOM institutionalize in-house DIB training. Such training should improve understanding of how these many different programs can be employed toward

DIB and how to integrate them with other security cooperation activities.

A Structured Approach to Support DIB Prioritization

Our analysis of DIB partner country selection found that prioritization is often ad hoc and based on informal sharing of opinions more than analysis. To help planners prioritize among countries within AFRI-COM's area of responsibility and to determine what types of DIB activities particular countries should receive, we present a structured approach to partner country selection based on publicly available country-level data. We use the Ibrahim Index of African Governance to provide information on partner nations' ability to absorb DIB programs, as well as a measure of the potential risks and likelihood of success of the DIB programs under consideration. The index uses about 100 indicators from over 30 independent African and global institutions to assess the quality of governance in African countries. Our approach is designed to provide a more objective analytical basis to facilitate the consultative prioritization process for AFRICOM DIB program planning without adding to the workload of DIB program directors. Although it should not serve as a replacement for current engagement prioritization processes, these metrics could enrich the dialogue among OSD, AFRICOM, and other stakeholders by adding additional analysis to discussions about partner selection and particular DIB activities. For instance, if a particular country has weak accountability scores, DoD may want to focus DIB efforts on making that country's defense finance systems more transparent.

Recommendation

Given the potential advantages of a more-analytic approach to DIB prioritization, we recommend that

- OSD and AFRICOM review their country analyses based on our approach in Chapter Three and consider incorporating similar analysis into their DIB decisionmaking processes.

Liberia and Libya Case Studies

The Liberia and Libya cases involved sweeping reforms—actual in Liberia's case, planned in Libya—to overhaul defense establishments and replace them with more efficient and accountable ones. Both had potential for great gains, but they were also high-risk efforts, particularly in Libya. In examining the two cases, common themes emerge. First, it is critical to have willing, capable, and engaged partner countries that are ready to invest their own resources in the effort. It is also imperative to match DIB ends to means and not establish overambitious goals that overwhelm a country's ability to absorb the help. Second, DIB-focused coordination should be institutionalized, both vertically (field level to headquarters) and horizontally. While coordination was reportedly effective in some cases, it remained ad hoc or driven by individual personalities in others. In future efforts, it will be important to establish coordination processes that overcome personality issues and survive staff rotations. A key process that requires bolstering is the integration of DIB tools into AFRICOM planning.

Recommendation

Given the potential value of a concerted effort to apply the DIB lessons described in our Liberia and Libya case studies, we recommend that

- OSD organize a pilot effort in a single African country to serve as a model for future DIB activities, including a five-year DIB plan developed by officials from OSD, the State Department, National Security Council staff, DSCA, AFRICOM, partner nation decisionmakers, and international partners. The plan would be based on a comprehensive baseline assessment conducted jointly with partner nation and international officials.

Conclusion

Looking across the full scope of our research, one overarching conclusion becomes clear. Because it requires different skills than most operationally and tactically focused engagements, effective DIB requires particularly close coordination at every level. Through the insights and recommendations discussed in the report, coordination—along with planning and implementation—should improve. These improvements should enable DIB to advance U.S. defense objectives in Africa more effectively than has been the case thus far.

Acknowledgments

Several people were instrumental in helping the authors produce this volume. The support provided included interviews (sometimes repeated interviews), documents, and feedback on our work. Among the people who supported our study, the authors especially thank the following people: Tommy Ross, Amanda Dory, Leslie Hunter, Todd Coker, David Cate, Pauline Kusiak, Matthew Minatelli, Aaron Jay, Juan Cardenas, Oz Sanborn, Jeanne Giraldo, Jeff Stefani, Ron Reynolds, Barbara Sotirin, Hap Harlow, Karsten Engelmann, and Michael Anderson.

In addition to the Defense DIB community, we received considerable assistance from several of our RAND colleagues: Walt Perry, Gillian Oak, Seth Jones, Laura Baldwin, Jerry Sollinger, Betsy Kammer, and Bryce Schoenborn. Finally, thanks to our reviewers, Stephen Watts and Douglas Lovelace, whose feedback greatly improved our report.

CHAPTER ONE

Introduction

Purpose

Defense institutions play two crucial roles in a country's defense sector. First, they sustain a country's military forces. Without the foundation of strong defense institutions, military forces will suffer from weak authorities and systems necessary for long-term effectiveness and responsiveness (e.g., administrative, legal, personnel, resource management, policy, strategy, logistics, and acquisition). Second, healthy defense institutions ensure military forces are professional, accountable, transparent, and subject to civilian oversight and the rule of law. Maintaining effective and legitimate defense institutions is challenging for all countries, but it can be particularly so in many African countries, where democratic governance, economic and social well-being, and security can be fragile. Despite the challenges, the 2014 Quadrennial Defense Review noted that in Africa, "there is also significant opportunity to develop stronger governance institutions and to help build professional, capable military forces that can partner with the United States to address the full spectrum of regional security challenges."[1] Our goal for this project was to assess DIB efforts in Africa and provide insights on possible improvements to planning and execution.

---

[1] U.S. Department of Defense (DoD), *Quadrennial Defense Review 2014*, Washington, D.C., 2014, p. 5.

Background: What Is DIB and Why Is It Relevant to Africa?

The draft DoD Directive on "Defense Institution Building (DIB)" defines DIB as "security cooperation activities with partner nations typically conducted at the ministerial, general, joint staff, military service headquarters and related defense agency level to improve defense governance and increase the sustainability of other DoD security cooperation programs."[2]

Defense institutions are "the people, organizations, rules, norms, values, and behaviors that enable oversight, governance, management, and functioning of the defense enterprise."[3] The goal of DIB to promote "effective, accountable, transparent, and responsive"[4] institutions is addressed through a variety of missions:

- improve the civilian control of armed forces
- transmit values of respect for the rule of law and human rights
- improve the management methods of defense institutions, as well as their support elements (most prominently: logistics, human resources, and financial management)
- professionalize defense personnel.

DIB can also be defined by what it is not: DIB does not target the operational readiness or tactical capabilities of partner nations, although readiness and capabilities will benefit from more-capable and accountable institutions.

A number of U.S. government actors engage in DIB. DoD is a major DIB provider through programs that include (but are not limited to) the Defense Institutional Reform Initiative (DIRI), the Defense Institute of International Legal Studies (DIILS), the Ministry of Defense Advisors Program (MoDA), and the regional centers for

---

[2]   Under Secretary of Defense for Policy, *Defense Institution Building (DIB)*, Draft Department of Defense Directive 5205.JB, Washington, D.C.: Department of Defense, as of May 11, 2015, p. 13.

[3]   Under Secretary of Defense for Policy, 2015, p. 13.

[4]   Under Secretary of Defense for Policy, 2015, p. 2.

security studies. Since DIB also aims at professionalizing defense personnel, any institution that engages in professional military education (PME)—as long as the students are officers or in a managerial position—is also part of the overall DIB enterprise. Another DIB provider is the U.S. State Department, whose Peacekeeping Operations program works to increase countries' capabilities to conduct peacekeeping operations and includes strengthening their institutional capacity.[5] Likewise, Global Peace Operations Initiative funds can be used to fulfill the objective of enhancing "the capacity of region/sub-regional organizations and institutions to train for, plan, deploy, manage, sustain, and obtain and integrate lessons learned from peace operations."[6] Beyond the U.S. government, other nations undertake DIB with their own partners, as do some international and regional organizations and nongovernmental organizations. For instance, the European Union's Integrated Border Assistance Mission has been assisting Libya in developing a national border-management strategy.[7]

The concept underlying DIB and its close relatives, security sector reform (SSR) and security sector governance (SSG), initially appeared in the 1990s in the wake of the collapse of the Soviet Union and the reform of Eastern and Central European defense sectors toward a model that reflected the best practices of the Euro-Atlantic community.

DIB is of particular relevance to Africa, where professionalization and accountability needs are immense. A report by the African Development Bank highlighted that only ten out of a sample of 51 African countries had never experienced a coup as of 2012.[8] Transparency International UK's Government Defense Anti-Corruption Index 2013 further shows that in Sub-Saharan Africa corruption risk in the

---

[5] U.S. Department of State, "Peacekeeping Operations (PKO)," web page, undated c.

[6] U.S. Department of State, "Global Peace Operations Initiative (GPOI) 'Phase II' (Fiscal Years 2010-2014)," web page, undated a.

[7] The mission began operating from Tunisia in August 2014, due to security constraints. See European Union External Action, "EU Integrated Border Assistance Mission in Libya (EUBAM Libya)," fact sheet, January 2015.

[8] Habiba Ben Barka and Mthuli Ncube, *Political Fragility in Africa: Are Military Coups d'Etat a Never-Ending Phenomenon?* African Development Bank, September 2012, p. 3.

defense sector is "high to critical," with little legislative oversight; there is little to no "evidence of serious engagement with civil society;" and there is a persistent lack of transparency of defense activities funding.[9] The challenges facing African militaries include lack of military professionalism, a high incidence of mutinies, human rights violations, complicity in illegal activities such as wildlife trafficking, politicization of the defense apparatus, and collusion with economic actors in profit-making ventures.[10]

Nevertheless, there is an opportunity for reform. Emile Ouédraogo, in his study of military professionalism in Africa, notes that

[a] majority of African states have duly adopted . . . democratic values and basic principles of military professionalism in their various constitutions and military doctrines. . . . [T]hese values are rooted in African culture. Protection of the kingdom, submission to the king, loyalty, and integrity vis-à-vis the community were core values of African ancestral warriors.[11]

Mali illustrates how military assistance can transition from episodic, operational support to more institutional efforts. In spite of the $60 million in counterterrorism funding it received from the United States since 2002,[12] in 2012 Mali saw its army promptly retreat before the advance of a coalition of secular and Islamist insurgent groups in the north, and President Amadou Toumani Touré was toppled by a military coup shortly thereafter. This debacle revealed how weak and unreliable the army as an institution—and the government as a whole—had been all along. Recent engagements with the Malian army, such as the efforts undertaken by the European Training Mis-

---

[9] Transparency International UK, "Sub-Saharan Africa," Government Defence Anti-Corruption Index 2013, undated.

[10] Emile Ouédraogo, *Advancing Military Professionalism in Africa*, Washington D.C.: Africa Center for Strategic Studies, Research Paper No. 6, July 2014, pp. 3, 4, 11, and 18–20.

[11] Ouédraogo, 2014, p. 5.

[12] Peter Tinti, "What Has the U.S. Already Tried in Mali?" *Christian Science Monitor*, November 20, 2012. Tinti notes that this figure is likely to be much higher due to the sensitive nature of some of the CT activities undertaken with this funding.

sion in Mali, have tried to follow a different model: "Rather than transferring knowledge and skills to individual soldiers, EU officers have helped the Malian Defense Ministry form new units from the ground up."[13] The next section provides more background on how the concept of DIB evolved over time and what best practices have been identified.

Approach

Our research objective was to assess how DoD was planning and executing DIB in Africa and to recommend ways to improve these efforts. Our approach was threefold. First, we analyzed past DIB-related SSR efforts and U.S. government guidance documents for Africa. Second, we reviewed the challenges of executing DIB programs in Africa. These challenges come in many forms, from translating DIB guidance into execution, to assessing DIB activities, to identifying DIB-related programs applicable to Africa, to prioritizing countries and activities. Third, we used a series of case studies to understand DIB from various perspectives. Our case studies included deep dives on how DIB was planned in two African countries, an analysis of the DoD regional centers as DIB providers, and through lessons from two U.S. allies that are also active in Africa: France and the United Kingdom. We chose to analyze Liberia because of the U.S. government's long history of DIB efforts there, whereas we chose Libya because of the intensive U.S. government DIB planning effort that took place from 2012 to 2014. In addition to these two primary case studies, we conducted a secondary case study on DoD's Africa Center for Strategic Studies (ACSS) and its Near East and South Asia Center for Strategic Studies (NESA) to analyze the relationship between PME efforts and DIB. We conducted our other secondary case studies—on French and British DIB efforts—so that we could draw insights from outside the U.S. government and so that we could assess DoD DIB activities against similar efforts by countries with long histories in Africa.

---

[13] Bruce Whitehouse, "How U.S. Military Assistance Failed in Mali," *Bridges from Bamako* blog post, April 21, 2014.

Our research team was able to analyze documents that ranged from presidential policy directives (PPDs), Defense Department guidance and policy memoranda, and the Defense Security Cooperation Agency's (DSCA's) budget reports to other strategic and national security and country plan guidance that would not have been possible without the assistance of several offices. As such, our team conducted over 50 interviews via telephone, email correspondence, and in-person visits with individuals in the following offices: the Office of the Secretary of Defense, U.S. Africa Command (AFRICOM), program management offices overseeing most DIB-related programs, NESA and ACSS, U.S. Department of State, UK Ministry of Defense, French Ministry of Defense, French Ministry of Foreign Affairs and International Development, and with members from the Africa Country Team Desk and United Nations Support Mission in Libya (UNSMIL).

The RAND database of DIB-related programs was built on the basis of two existing security cooperation databases, the *Army Security Cooperation Handbook*, and a 2013 RAND report on security cooperation mechanisms used by combatant commands.[14] After removing funding sources and authorities to keep only programs in the database, and removing those programs that were no longer active or did not engage in DIB efforts, we were left with 47 Africa-relevant DIB programs, which we further categorized in three types, based on their focus and type of activities: defense management, defense professionalization, and defense familiarization. These different categories allowed for a more-nuanced analysis of how existing security cooperation programs support DIB.

How This Report Is Organized

The remainder of this report contains four chapters and three appendices. Chapter Two describes DIB, why it is relevant to Africa, and

---

[14] U.S. Department of the Army, *Army Security Cooperation Handbook*, Washington, D.C., Pamphlet 11-31, March 5, 2013b; Jennifer D. P. Moroney, David E. Thaler, and Joe Hogler, *Review of Security Cooperation Mechanisms Combatant Commands Utilize to Build Partner Capacity*, Santa Monica, Calif.: RAND Corporation, RR-413-OSD, 2013.

how it fits in with U.S. strategic objectives. Chapter Three discusses some of the challenges involved with carrying out DIB in Africa and suggests some potential ways of overcoming these challenges. Chapter Four contains two DIB case studies: Liberia and Libya. Chapter Five presents our conclusions and recommendations. Appendix A describes AFRICOM's assessment process. Appendix B discusses how DoD's regional centers contribute to the DIB effort in Africa. Finally, Appendix C discusses the experiences of two allies, France and the United Kingdom, in DIB-like efforts in Africa.

CHAPTER TWO

DIB Best Practices and Their Relevance to U.S. Strategic Objectives in Africa

The concepts underlying DIB are not new. As the institutional dimension of broader SSR, DIB efforts have been going on for several decades. The history of DIB shows how such reform efforts picked up pace after the end of the Cold War, and how some major examples of DIB took place in Africa. This DIB experience has resulted in a collection of lessons, as well as best practices, that can inform present efforts. Such efforts directly serve U.S. strategic objectives in Africa, either directly, by building accountable and effective defense forces, or indirectly, by creating the conditions that make it possible for partner nations to provide for their own security, export security through participation in peacekeeping missions, and counter extremism and other violent threats within their borders.

DIB: History and Purpose

At the June 2004 Istanbul Summit, the North Atlantic Treaty Organization (NATO) adopted a Partnership Action Plan on Defence Institution Building. The purpose of this partnership was to "build democratically responsible defence institutions."[1] NATO, until recently, was the main user of the term. As a result, most of the literature on DIB focuses on European countries.[2]

---

[1] NATO, "Istanbul Summit Communiqué," press release, June 28, 2004.

[2] Leonid Polyakov, for instance, examined the history and different stages of DIB in Ukraine from 1991 to 2008. See Leonid I. Polyakov, "Defense Institution Building in

9

The concept behind DIB—promoting capable, transparent, and accountable defense institutions—has been widespread since the 1990s, when Western governments engaged the Central and Eastern European countries that had emerged from communist rule to improve their civil-military relations. It was during that decade that it "became increasingly accepted that democratic governance of the security sector is essential to security."[3] The same Western governments also saw DIB as a way to protect development assistance from predatory state institutions.[4]

SSG is a term that predates DIB but encompasses most of its definition. SSG involves improving management of security bodies, enhancing accountability, and improving their professionalism.[5] Under its "Security Sector Governance" section, for instance, the United States Institute of Peace "helps to build professional, sustainable, and locally supported security institutions that promote democracy and the rule of law by assisting U.S. and foreign governments in reforming security sector institutions and developing a cadre of experts through education and training."[6] This is similar to the DIB mission, though it typically extends beyond Ministry of Defense–controlled forces to other armed security forces, such as national police and armed border guards. The Organisation for Economic Co-operation and Development's (OECD) Development Assistance Committee handbook on SSR, which stands as an international reference on this issue, also uses the term *capacity development*, in opposition to "training and technical assistance approaches."[7] Describing a mission similar to DIB's, capacity

Ukraine," *Connections: The Quarterly Journal*, Vol. 7, No. 2, 2008, pp. 15–20.

[3]   Nicole Ball, "Reforming Security Sector Governance," *Conflict, Security & Development*, Vol. 4, No. 3, 2004, pp. 510–511.

[4]   Heiner Hänngi and Fred Tanner, "Promoting Security Sector Governance in the EU's Neighbourhood," *Chaillot Paper*, No. 80, European Union Institute for Security Studies, July 2005, p. 11.

[5]   Ball, 2004, p. 511.

[6]   United States Institute of Peace, "Security Sector Governance," web page, undated.

[7]   OECD, *OECD DAC Handbook on Security System Reform: Supporting Security and Justice*, Paris: OECD Publishing, February 2007a, p. 86.

development "is closely linked with the governance agenda and efforts to improve institutions, laws, incentives, transparency and leadership."[8]

The most frequently encountered term, however, is SSR, along with the slightly narrower *defense sector reform*. If SSG is the objective to be pursued, SSR is the main instrument with which to pursue it.[9] For instance, the Geneva Center for the Democratic Control of Armed Forces—established in 2000 by the Swiss Confederation—aims at "enhancing security sector governance (SSG) through security sector reform (SSR)."[10] SSR is broader than DIB, for it encompasses all security institutions, not only those in charge of defense. SSR recipients may include national police forces, armed border guards, the justice system, penitentiary institutions, and non-state security providers such as local mediation mechanisms.[11] As a result, the four terms (security sector governance, capacity development, SSR, and defense sector reform) are closely related but not synonyms.[12]

However, SSR remains the term of choice for two reasons. First, the security sector is generally seen as the sum of different parts that closely interact, suggesting that little benefit accrues from addressing only one (defense) while leaving all the others (national police, border guards, etc.) in a state of dysfunction. Second, lessons learned from improving the governance of defense institutions often have relevance

---

[8]   OECD, 2007a, p. 86.

[9]   Hänngi and Tanner, 2005, p. 11.

[10]   Geneva Center for the Democratic Control of Armed Forces, "Who We Are," web page, undated.

[11]   See, for instance, a list of types of actors influencing SSG in Nicole J. Ball, Kayode Fayemi, Funmi Olonisakin, Martin Rupiya, and Rocklyn Williams, "Governance in the Security Sector," in Nicolas van de Walle, Nicole Ball, and Vijaya Ramachandran (eds.), *Beyond Structural Adjustment: The Institutional Context of African Development*, New York: Palgrave Macmillan, 2003, pp. 263–304.

[12]   African scholars and practitioners have supported the use of a fifth term: security sector transformation (SST). SST supposedly promotes changes more radical than mere "reform." This concept gained inspiration from the case of South Africa, which saw a major overhaul of its defense institutions following the end of apartheid, but does not seem to have gained much traction in recent years, as SSR remained the term of choice (Alan Bryden and Fummi Olonisakin, eds., *Security Sector Transformation in Africa*, Munster: LIT Verlag, 2010, pp. 3, 7 and 9).

for other security institutions. Consequently, it makes sense, when reflecting on reform, to consider the security sector as a whole. To summarize, defense sector reform and DIB are largely similar, and SSR encompasses them both in a way that makes lessons and good practices of SSR of direct relevance to DIB (see Figure 2.1).

A number of bilateral and multilateral actors have played a key role in the development of SSR since the 1990s. The Netherlands and the United Kingdom were precursors in this regard.[13] On the multilateral side, organizations conduct a variety of programs dedicated to SSR, including the OECD; the World Bank; NATO; and, within the UN family, the United Nations Development Programme (UNDP) and the Department of Peacekeeping Operations.[14] Some of these organizations have issued key documents that provide guidance on SSR. The earliest ones are the Organization for Security and Co-operation in Europe's 1994 Code of Conduct on Politico-Military Aspects of Secu-

Figure 2.1
Security Sector Governance: SSR/DIB Interaction

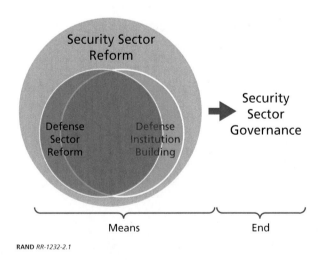

RAND RR-1232-2.1

---

[13] Ball, 2004, pp. 510 and 521.

[14] Hänngi and Tanner, 2005, p. 21. For more on each of these institutions, see same, pp. 22–26.

rity and NATO's Partnership for Peace (PfP) program.[15] In 2002, the UNDP's *Human Development Report* provided a list of key principles of democratic governance in the security sector.[16] In the United States, guidance on SSR issued jointly by the U.S. Agency for International Development, Department of State, and DoD in 2009—coupled with the more-recent PPD 23, issued in 2013—have informed SSR developments and doctrine.[17] Army doctrine, such as Field Manual 3-22, *Army Support to Security Cooperation*, is also an important source of guidance.[18]

In Africa, the African Union (AU) developed its own *Policy Framework on Security Sector Reform*, based on consultations with member states and SSR experts. This framework builds on other well-established SSR best practices adapted to the African context.[19] In addition to the principles already developed by the AU and the United Nations on SSR, the framework incorporates additional elements that are deemed to be "values that are particularly relevant for or unique to the African continent."[20] These values are African solidarity and African partnerships; including SSR in regional integration on peace and security; national ownership, national responsibility, and national commitment;

---

[15] Heiner Hänngi, *The Challenges of Security Sector Governance*, Geneva Center for the Democratic Control of Armed Forces, 2003, pp. 12–13.

[16] UNDP, *Human Development Report 2002: Deepening Democracy in a Fragmented World*, New York: Oxford University Press, 2002, p. 90.

[17] U.S. Agency for International Development, U.S. Department of Defense, and U.S. Department of State, *Security Sector Reform*, Washington, D.C., February 2009. The White House, "Fact Sheet: U.S. Security Sector Assistance Policy," Presidential Policy Directive 23, April 2013. In addition, Ball, 2004 (p. 521), highlights the work done by DoD's regional centers, the Department of Justice, and the Expanded International Military Education and Training program. SSR is also part of U.S. Army doctrine, which cites it as "an aspect of stability operations" (see U.S. Department of the Army, *Stability Operations*, Field Manual 3-07, October 2008.

[18] U.S. Department of the Army, *Army Support to Security Cooperation*, Field Manual 3-22, January 2013a, pp. 1–12. See also Joint Chiefs of Staff, *Security Force Assistance*, Joint Doctrine Note 1-13, April 29, 2013.

[19] African Union Commission, *African Union Policy Framework on Security Sector Reform*, Addis Ababa, Ethiopia, undated.

[20] African Union Commission, undated, Section B, para. 15–16.

national vision for SSR (to guide external support); making SSR context-specific; including informal and customary security providers and traditional justice actors; integrating SSR in a broader democratization and reform process; respecting good governance; abiding by the principles of gender equality and women's empowerment; and ensuring coordination of SSR assistance.[21] Other key AU documents on SSR include the AU's "Common African Defense and Security Policy," the "Framework for an African Union Response to Unconstitutional Changes," the Southern African Development Community's "Strategic Indicative Plan for the Organ on Politics, Defense and Security Cooperation," and the Economic Community of West African States (ECOWAS)'s "Draft Code of Conduct for Armed and Security Forces."[22] These documents underline the need to address some of the common challenges that a large number of defense institutions experience across Africa.[23] Ouédraogo, in his 2014 ACSS report, pointed to the institutional factors—"gaps in the chain of command leading to indiscipline, inadequate oversight of procurement practices, weak resource management diminishing operational capacity, poor morale, and a misaligned or obsolete mission"—that undermine the operational capacity of most African militaries.[24]

Three types of DIB stand out from SSR practice. These are listed in Figure 2.2.

First, DIB can be done through large-scale, sweeping reforms that overhaul defense establishments and replace them with more efficient and accountable ones. This type of reform typically takes place in post-conflict countries, where most institutions—the defense sector included—need to be rebuilt from the ground up. These efforts are particularly challenging because of the amount of resources and time

---

[21] African Union Commission, undated, Section B, para. 16.

[22] Ouédraogo, 2014, pp. 14–15. For more on ECOWAS's action on SSR, see Okey Uzoechina, *Security Sector Reform and Governance Processes in West Africa: From Concepts to Reality*, Geneva Center for the Democratic Control of Armed Forces, Policy Paper No. 35, 2014.

[23] Ouédraogo, 2014, p. 15.

[24] Ouédraogo, 2014, p. 22.

Figure 2.2
Three Main Types of DIB Efforts

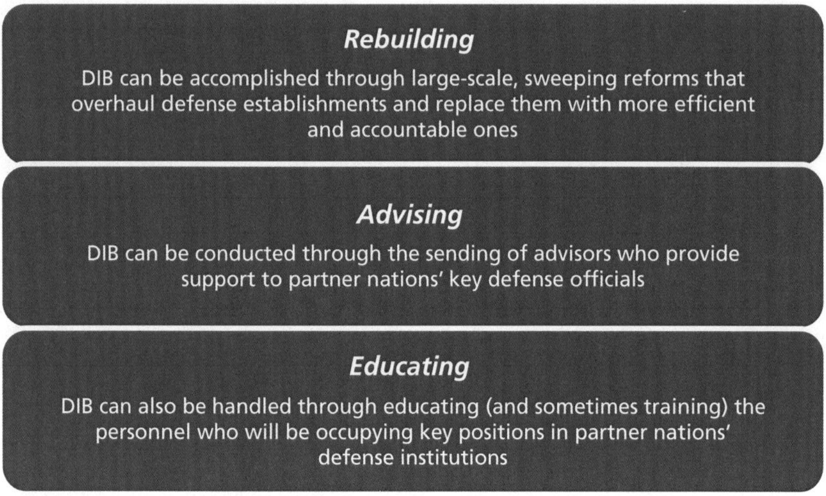

Rebuilding
DIB can be accomplished through large-scale, sweeping reforms that overhaul defense establishments and replace them with more efficient and accountable ones

Advising
DIB can be conducted through the sending of advisors who provide support to partner nations' key defense officials

Educating
DIB can also be handled through educating (and sometimes training) the personnel who will be occupying key positions in partner nations' defense institutions

RAND *RR-1232-2.2*

required, but they have the potential for transformational influence, precisely because these are areas of "least resistance where state capacity is limited and thus external actors are able to penetrate the system without dealing with recalcitrant gatekeeping elites who presided over repressive and collapsed systems."[25]

Second, DIB can be done by sending advisors who provide support to partner nations' key defense officials. Advisors assess what defense processes can be improved and offer advice on how to fix inefficiencies. The effect of such efforts depends, in large part, on the quality of the advisory team and is contingent on the willingness of officials in the partner nation to act on the recommendations it receives. As with the United States, partner governments consist of individual actors with different levels of authority and abilities and a variety of views. Some will feel ownership of an issue, and others will not. Thus, part of the job of advisors can also be to assess which local actors have the ability

---

[25] Bryden and Olonisakin, 2010, p. 11.

Box 1
Rebuilding Defense Institutions in Post-Conflict Settings: The Examples of Sierra Leone and Liberia

The United Kingdom played a key role in rebuilding the defense institutions of Sierra Leone after the 1991–2002 war. The UK's International Military Advisory and Assistance Team reformed the Ministry of Defense and replaced military officers with civilians in a number of top positions. They also improved transparency through better communication and closer work with local communities.[1] The Sierra Leonean army was downsized by almost 50 percent and restructured. Its personnel policy (including recruitment, pay, and pensions) was entirely reformed as well—a necessary step to ensure that the composition of the army would adequately reflect the Sierra Leonean nation rather than being a tool of power controlled by a particular regional or ethnic group.[2] The UK, through its Department for International Development (DfID), also worked on improving the parliament's capacity to oversee defense forces.[3]

The United States undertook a similarly large-scale reform effort in Liberia following the 1989–2003 war, which killed an estimated 250,000 people and displaced and mutilated many more. The 2003 Comprehensive Peace Agreement mandated the reconstruction of the Armed Forces of Liberia.[4] Deemed in 2009 a "provisional success" by the International Crisis Group, the U.S. effort focused on downsizing of the army, recruitment and vetting of new soldiers, and basic training.[5] The SSR program in Liberia also included constructing bases across the country, establishing a professional defense ministry, drafting a national defense strategy, and designing a new force structure.[6] Liberia represents the most comprehensive U.S. defense sector reform effort to have taken place in Africa.

---

[1]   Jeremy Ginifer, "The Challenges of the Security Sector and Security Reform Processes in Democratic Transitions: The Case of Sierra Leone," *Democratization*, Vol. 13, No. 5, 2006, pp. 800–801.

[2]   Ginifer, 2006, p. 800.

[3]   Ginifer, 2006, p. 802.

[4]   On defense sector reform in Liberia, see, for instance, David C. Gompert, Olga Oliker, Brooke Stearns Lawson, Keith Crane, and K. Jack Reilly, *Making Liberia Safe: Transformation of the National Security Sector*, Santa Monica, Calif.: RAND Corporation, MG-529-OSD, 2007, and Alix Julia Boucher, *Defense Sector Reform: A Note on Current Practice*, Henry L. Stimson Center, December 12, 2009, pp. 13–23.

[5]   International Crisis Group, *Liberia: Uneven Progress in Security Sector Reform*, Crisis Group Africa Report No. 148, January 13, 2009, p. 11. For a detailed account of the United States' SSR efforts in Liberia, see Sean McFate, *Building Better Armies: An Insider's Account of Liberia*, Carlisle Barracks, Penn.: U.S. Army War College, Strategic Studies Institute and Peacekeeping and Stabilization Operations Institute, 2013.

[6]   John Blaney, Jacques Paul Klein, and Sean McFate, *Wider Lessons for Peacebuilding: Security Sector Reform in Liberia*, Muscatine, Ia.: The Stanley Foundation, June 2010, p. 6.

and willingness to implement improvements and how to convert political will into action.

Third, DIB can also be done through educating (and sometimes training) the personnel who will be occupying key positions in partner nations' defense institutions. The United States and its Western European allies have long been involved in such activities through PME programs. The leading U.S. program is the Department of State's International Military Education and Training (IMET) program, which funds military and civilian personnel from U.S. partner nations to attend U.S. PME institutions, typically for one year. Included in the IMET program's mission statement is the goal to "improve host nation ability to manage its defense establishment."[26] Since 1990, the Expanded International Military Education and Training objectives further detail the ways in which to foster this ability to manage defense establishments, including

> . . . contributing to responsible defense resource management; fostering respect for and understanding of democracy and civilian rule of law, including the principle of civilian control of the military; contributing to cooperation between military and law enforcement personnel with respect to counternarcotics law enforcement efforts; and improving the military justice system and promoting an awareness and understanding of internationally recognized human rights.[27]

In fiscal year (FY) 2015, $107 million were requested for the IMET program. About 12 percent of that amount went to Africa (up from an estimated 9 percent in FY 2014), which is on par with the amounts devoted to South and Central Asia, East Asia and the Pacific, and the Western Hemisphere. Africa's share comes far behind Europe

---

[26] DSCA, *Security Assistance Management Manual*, April 30, 2012, para. C10.6.1 and C10.6.3.1.

[27] DSCA, 2012, para. C10.6.3.2.

and Eurasia (about 27 percent), as well as the Near East (about 18 percent).[28]

DIB Lessons from Recent History

During the approximately 20 years that SSR and SSG have been important elements of U.S. national security strategy, practitioners have gathered and recorded an archive of lessons learned and best practices. This section examines several of them.

The first lesson is the need to tailor SSR and DIB to the specific conditions of the partner. This includes the imperative to understand how their national security institutions function, who the key players are, and how they interact with each other.[29] The U.S. Army field manual on security cooperation also highlights this element and states that one of the foundations of SSR is a "concept of security developed by the host nation and ingrained in its culture," as the "SSR plan reflects host-nation culture, sensitivities, and historical conceptions of security."[30] More generally, practitioners have warned that SSR is a challenging undertaking. This also means that SSR and, by extension, DIB are unlikely to show quick results. It is typically a "social process that may take a long, complex and uneven path."[31]

Another lesson is the difficulty of creating lasting change through discrete interventions, since all institutions interact and, to a certain extent, rely on each other. As Ball put it, "The security sector cannot be an island of probity in a sea of misconduct."[32] Similarly, the defense sector is unlikely to be efficient and accountable if the rest of the security sector (e.g., police, justice) is not. This, however, should not deter outside countries from undertaking DIB and other reforms, since

---

[28] U.S. Department of State, "International Military Education and Training Account Summary," web page, undated b.

[29] Ball, 2004, p. 519.

[30] U.S. Department of the Army, 2013a.

[31] Hänngi, 2003, p. 17.

[32] Ball, 2004, p. 513.

the defense sector often can lead the initiation of broader governance reforms.

> The lesson from governance reform is that even modest injections of transparency can yield benefits. . . . Increased transparency strengthens the hand of formal democratic institutions such as parliament and the judiciary. It also unleashes the potential for civil society and the media to strengthen civil accountability and control by scrutinizing security budgets, providing technical input and opening security policies to public debate.[33]

Past practice also points to a number of elements that can facilitate SSR and DIB to increase its chances of success. Ball cites commitment of the leadership, ensuring that the new institutions reflect the country's history and culture, and fostering consultations within the government and between the government and civil society.[34] Hänggi and Tanner acknowledge that reforms should be adapted to the specific contexts of the countries in which they apply, but also identify three "context clusters" based on socio-economic development, the political system, and the security situation, which warrant common lessons. They find that "Good opportunities for externally assisted SSR activities tend to exist in developing countries which have embarked on a process of democratization after elections or other forms of peaceful change, in post-authoritarian transition states which aim at joining a regional organization for which democracy is a requirement for membership (e.g., potential EU and NATO members), and those post-conflict states in which multinational peace support operations offer the bases for reconstruction and local actors show a certain readiness for reform." These authors, however, see "dim" prospects for SSR in "authoritarian regimes and illiberal democracies where the will to reform is lacking . . . and to 'post-conflict' states and territories located in early conflict transformation phases."[35]

---

[33] *Human Development Report 2002*, pp. 90–91.

[34] Ball, 2004, p. 513.

[35] Hänngi and Tanner, 2005, p. 18.

The latter contexts offer lesser chances of success for reform efforts, as well as higher risks.[36] There are a number of reasons that the U.S. government might pursue DIB and other types of reform despite long odds of success. DIB planners must develop a variety of options while ensuring decisions are based on clear and objective analysis.

Finally, a key lesson learned from two decades of SSR practice is the importance of implementation. Reform efforts should focus both on what new institutions or policies are put in place and how they are implemented. This requires a program of regular assessments, monitoring, and evaluation of a series of sustained engagements, rather than episodic events that terminate before implementation is well on its way.[37] As a result, SSR is a protracted effort, which often requires large investments and a comprehensive, multiyear approach that emphasizes the long-term sustainability of the reforms. Such needs have been highlighted repeatedly in international forums and best practices documents, including the OECD's 2007 "Principles for Good International Engagement in Fragile States and Situations," which commands in its ninth principle to "Act fast . . . but stay engaged long enough to give success a chance."[38] A number of academic works, too, highlighted that donors should not expect quick returns on their SSR investments and need to make long-term commitments.[39]

---

[36] Hänngi and Tanner, 2005, pp. 17–18.

[37] Ball, 2004, p. 519.

[38] OECD, "Principles for Good International Engagement in Fragile States and Situations," April 2007b.

[39] For instance, Lant Pritchett, Michael Woolcock, and Matt Andrews, *Capability Traps? The Mechanisms of Persistent Implementation Failure*, Washington, D.C.: Center for Global Development, Working Paper 234, December 2010, offers sobering conclusions on what can be expected in terms of end results for some of the countries with the worst governance indicators, even under the best circumstances. We are indebted to our colleague Steve Watts for pointing this reference to us. See also Nicole Ball and Michael Brzoska, with Kees Kingma and Herbert Wulf, "Voice and Accountability in the Security Sector," Bonn International Center for Conversion, Paper 21, July 2002, p. 48.

How Is DIB Relevant to U.S. Strategic Objectives in Africa?

DIB efforts can play a significant role in furthering U.S. strategic objectives in Africa, as evidenced by a survey of U.S. government strategic guidance documents pertaining to Africa (see Table 2.1). We also included documents that provided indications as to how key U.S. government actors understood this guidance or planned to implement

Table 2.1
Africa-Related Documents Surveyed

Document Type	Document Name or Source
Strategic guidance	PPD 13, PPD 16, PPD 23, 2010 National Security Strategy, 2012 Defense Strategic Guidance, and the State Department's Joint Regional Strategy for Africa[a]
Implementation guidance	Annual AFRICOM commander posture statements (2008 to 2013)
Other sources	DSCA budget reports; U.S. Government Accountability Office reports; military, congressional, and academic publications from the Army's Knowledge Online Center for Army Lessons Learned databases[b]

SOURCES: The White House, "Political and Economic Reform in the Middle East and North Africa," Presidential Policy Directive 13, undated; The White House, *U.S. Strategy for Sub-Saharan Africa*, Presidential Policy Directive 16, June 2012; The White House, 2013; The White House, *National Security Strategy*, Washington, D.C., May 2010; DoD, *Sustaining U.S. Global Leadership: Priorities for 21st Century Defense*, Washington, D.C., January 2012; U.S. Africa Command Public Affairs, "AFRICOM Posture Statement: Ward Updates Congress on U.S. Africa Command," Annual Testimony to Congress, March 13, 2008; William E. Ward, "United States Africa Command: 2009 Posture Statement," U.S. Africa Command Public Affairs Office, Annual Testimony to Congress, March 2009; U.S. Africa Command Public Affairs, "AFRICOM Posture Statement: Ward Reports Annual Testimony to Congress," Annual Testimony to Congress, March 9, 2010; Carter Ham, *USAFRICOM Posture Statement*, 2011, 2012, and 2013.

[a] We were, however, unable to view all of the integrated country strategies (ICSs) nested under the Joint Regional Strategy. As of July 2014, country-specific ICSs were unavailable for many of the DIB-heavy countries and were still forthcoming.

[b] The following documents were consulted: Lauren Ploch, *Africa Command: U.S. Strategic Interests and the Role of the U.S. Military in Africa*, Washington, D.C.: Congressional Research Service, RL34003, January 5, 2009, and July 22, 2011; William B. Garrett III, "Forward in Africa: USAFRICAOM and the U.S. Army in Africa," web page, U.S. Army Africa, January 10, 2010; Edward Marks, "Why USAFRICOM?" *Joint Forces Quarterly*, Vol. 52, January 2009; and Philip Seib and Carola Weil, "AFRICOM, the American Military and Public Diplomacy in Africa," USC Annenberg Policy Briefing, March 2008.

it (e.g., the commander of U.S. Africa Command's [AFRICOM's] annual posture statements), as well as military, congressional, and academic publications focusing specifically on DIB and security cooperation objectives in Africa.

We looked specifically for Africa-related objectives in the U.S. government strategic and implementation guidance. This search retrieved 48 different Africa-related objectives. A survey of the "other sources" listed in Table 2.1 did not uncover any additional objectives. The 48 objectives presented some important similarities, and could be further clustered into six core objectives, presented in Table 2.2.

Objectives 3 and 6 directly affect several other strategic objectives. Effective security institutions, as well as professional and accountable military forces, provide the conditions that make it possible to deter extremism and combat transnational threats. They create a virtuous circle by reinforcing the country's ability to provide security to its citizens and the region as a whole (see Figure 2.3). For instance, legitimate and accountable security institutions reduce the risk of abuses against the civilian population and repression of ethnic and religious minorities that can provide fertile ground for radicalization and extremism, whether homegrown or transnational (Objectives 4 and 5). It also

Table 2.2
U.S. Strategic Objectives for Africa

Objectives
1. African countries/organizations provide for their own security.
2. African countries have a peace operation capacity to contribute to security on the continent.
3. **African countries have capable and accountable military forces that perform professionally and with integrity.**
4. African governments/regional security organizations possess the capability to mitigate the threat of violent extremism.
5. African governments and organizations have the capability to dissuade, deter, and defeat transnational threats.
6. **African military forces are supported and sustained by effective, legitimate, and professional security institutions.**

NOTE: The two U.S. objectives in boldface are directly linked to DIB.

Figure 2.3
U.S. DIB Objectives Serve as Stepping Stones to Other Strategic Objectives

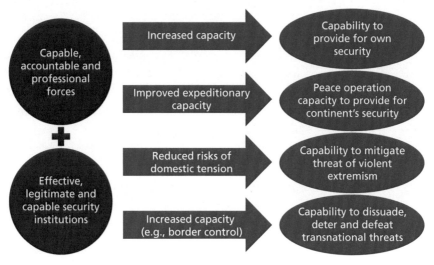

RAND *RR-1232-2.3*

increases a partner nation's own security, by reducing internal tensions, and its legitimacy in providing security to its neighbors (Objectives 1 and 2). In this way, DIB objectives are directly or indirectly supporting key U.S. strategic objectives in Africa.

The best practices gathered over many years of defense sector reform efforts, including DIB, can inform ongoing programs in Africa. Two key U.S. strategic objectives for the region overlap with DIB, underscoring the importance of this type of engagement in Africa. The potential impact of DIB efforts on partner nations' security goes even further, as successfully reforming defense institutions can be expected to have positive ripple effects on partner nations' ability to stay secure, export security, contain violent extremism, and deter transnational threats—all U.S. strategic objectives for Africa. Despite its importance, our document reviews and interviews indicated that planners and implementers often fail to understand these important linkages between DIB objectives and other U.S. objectives. Part of this failure stems in part from the fact that there is limited written guidance and other documents to help stakeholders truly understand DIB (as well as SSR) and implement it effectively.

Even more challenging than limited guidance are the structural constraints that inhibit the United States from applying best practices through sufficiently robust and effective DIB. For example, the significant mismatch between resources required and those available (including outside DoD) prevents the United States from implementing SSR and DIB within ideal parameters. There is also a mismatch between the long timelines required for SSR and DIB to take hold and the extremely short (usually one year) funding cycles of most U.S. programs. Finally, the stovepiped nature of congressional authorities makes it almost impossible to implement a comprehensive, whole-of-government approach. Because the scale of these challenges can seem overwhelming, our report focuses primarily on small, concrete steps DoD officials can implement relatively quickly and easily.

CHAPTER THREE

DIB Programs in Africa: Challenges and Responses

As the previous chapter showed, strengthening defense institutions is, in many ways, the foundation for most other U.S. security objectives in Africa. Our research indicates, however, that DIB is especially challenging in Africa, given the prevalence of fragile states and political sensitivities about sovereignty. In this chapter, we analyze these challenges and discuss ways DoD can strengthen its ability to identify and apply DIB programs in Africa.

From DIB Guidance to Execution: The Roles of OSD, AFRICOM, and African Partners

To understand the challenges of DIB in Africa, we started with three questions. First, what do Office of the Secretary of Defense (OSD) policymakers want? Second, what do planners at AFRICOM need? And third, what will African partners accept? Although other U.S. government and international actors play an important role in DIB, we focus here on the distribution of interests, challenges, and roles across the DoD and African partners.

What OSD Policymakers Want

As discussed in Chapter One, we analyzed a wide array of DoD documents and interviewed officials involved in U.S. policymaking for Africa, as well as officials responsible for security cooperation programs worldwide. DoD policymakers see DIB as a way to ensure defense institutions in partner nations have the skills and professionalism to oversee their countries' military forces. Without capable, transparent, and accountable defense institutions, the militaries that defense officials manage could suffer from ineffective civilian oversight, unsustainability, weakened rule of law, and inadequate human rights protections.

U.S. military assistance to Africa illustrates this concern well. Counterterrorism requirements helped to almost triple funding under DoD authorities from 2009 to 2014. Policymakers in the State Department, OSD, and elsewhere were concerned that, without a proper balance between investments in institutional capacity and operational/ tactical improvements, U.S. efforts to train and equip partner nations in Africa might produce more operationally capable but not more professional or sustainable forces.[1]

Many policymakers in OSD want a top-down approach to institution building. Such an approach is valuable for two reasons. First, because institutions are located at the headquarters level and closer to powerful decisionmakers, working with them may be more politically sensitive than, say, training an army battalion. Engagement must therefore carefully reflect strategic guidance from the White House, State Department, and senior DoD leaders. Second, the best sources of talent for strengthening partner institutions are often current or former officials from institutions in the United States that have counterparts in the African nation. For example, civil servants in the human resources and budget components of African ministries of defense or military service headquarters may benefit more from engagements with Americans with similar experience than with military operators. Thus, in general, OSD staff members are more familiar with the former, and combatant command staffs with the latter. Simply put, OSD policymakers involved in security cooperation and in Africa generally want more control over DIB compared with most other security cooperation programs, which are controlled to a greater degree by combatant commands.

Combatant commands have well-established processes for integrating top-down guidance and bottom-up demand signals from U.S. embassy country teams into their planning. But combatant commands are ultimately operational staffs, so integrating the intensive top-down

---

[1]   Interviews with DoD officials, April and July 2014 and February 2015.

management approach that effective DIB implementation may require can be challenging. This may be particularly true in Africa, where counterterrorism and other operational concerns are high and institutional capacity is often low. Some officials worry about OSD setting overly ambitious professionalization goals and wasting resources on poorly planned initiatives.[2] Others, however, emphasize that past experiences have led to development of several best practices that are improving planning and avoiding such pitfalls. For example, DoD planners are expected to focus on "fertile ground," i.e., those organizations within partner institutions where there already exists some degree of willingness and ability to improve performance. Also, rather than trying to impose U.S. values, DIB implementers aim to expose partners to these values while focusing primarily on developing professionals with a technocratic, apolitical, transparent, and analytic approach.

Some officials also expressed concern that OSD guidance is not well understood and perhaps even resisted among AFRICOM staff and other stakeholders involved with DIB efforts in Africa.[3] Some stakeholders misperceived DIB as focused only on advising ministers of defense. Others argued that institutions included the leadership and staff of operational military units, such as army brigades, and that focusing at this level would produce more-concrete results. Still others were confused about roles and responsibilities among OSD staff and DIB program managers. Despite evidence of extensive communication efforts, these exchanges were often ad hoc and reactive, whereas a more systematic and strategic dialogue could improve understanding and buy-in from AFRICOM and U.S. embassy planners and other stakeholders. To get what it wants in Africa, OSD may require better marketing of DIB tools. OSD's establishment of a DIB Coordination Board should prove helpful, as it can facilitate communication across DoD.[4]

Another factor contributing to the challenge of top-down/bottom-up integration is that DSCA has a role that is unclear to many stakeholders. DSCA has full program management authority for most

---

[2]   Interviews with DoD officials, April and July 2014.

[3]   Interviews with DoD officials, April and July 2014 and February 2015.

[4]   Under Secretary of Defense for Policy, 2015.

U.S. government security cooperation activities implemented by DoD, but the degree of management it can exercise over DIB programs is complicated and confusing.[5] DSCA plays a crucial role integrating the thousands of security cooperation activities executed each year. It educates security cooperation professionals around the world through its Defense Institute of Security Assistance Management. DSCA's staff communicates with these professionals on a daily basis. In addition to clarifying DSCA's role through written guidance, OSD leaders should use the DIB Coordination Board to ensure that guidance on roles and responsibilities is clearly understood.

What AFRICOM Planners Need

As part of our research, we interviewed a cross section of officials from AFRICOM and reviewed AFRICOM planning documents to discover what AFRICOM planners really need. In one sense, the answer to this question is simple: clearly articulated requirements. But who articulates DIB requirements and how is it challenging? Because combatant commands are operational organizations, planners can sometimes approach security cooperation as a bottom-up effort. For example, planners might start with improving the capabilities of an army company and then aim two levels up to strengthen a brigade. Institutions are sometimes viewed to include brigade staff headquarters, logistics units, and other units that enable and sustain combat units.

DIB can also become a type of "miscellaneous" category for activities that do not fit anywhere else. For example, in 2013 and 2014, AFRICOM's leadership expressed an interest in dedicating about one-third of its resources toward DIB. As the shaded row in Table 3.1 shows, this goal was almost achieved, but only by including programs relating to HIV/AIDS, humanitarian demining (i.e., post-conflict landmine removal), and pandemic response. Simply by removing HIV/AIDS programs, AFRICOM's resources aligned with DIB dropped from 29 percent to 5 percent. Even tracking what resources

---

[5]   For a more detailed discussion of this issue, see Walter L. Perry, Stuart E. Johnson, Stephanie Pezard, Gillian S. Oak, David Stebbins, and Chaoling Feng, *Defense Institution Building: An Assessment*, Santa Monica, Calif.: RAND Corporation, RR-1176-OSD, forthcoming.

Table 3.1
Resources Dedicated to AFRICOM Activities

AFRICOM Lines of Effort	FY 2014 Resources (Percentage of Total)
Counter violent extremist organizations	$278 million 50%
Strengthen defense institutions	$162 million ($27 million w/o HIV/AIDS) 29% (5% w/o HIV/AIDS)
Peacekeeping operations and crisis response	$63 million 11%
Assured access and freedom of movement	$33 million 6%
Counter illicit trafficking	$10 million 2%
Maritime security	$9 million 2%

SOURCE: Spreadsheets provided to RAND by AFRICOM J5.

were authorized for DIB compared with what was actually spent was challenging. The assignment of a DIB coordinator in 2014 and organization of a DIB conference in 2015 alleviated some of AFRICOM's challenges in understanding and responding to DIB requirements, but it will take several years for a coordinator and conferences to institutionalize best practices.

To understand requirements, AFRICOM also needs a solid foundation of security cooperation planning and assessments in which to embed DIB efforts. Planning documents, along with stakeholder conferences, can be important coordination mechanisms, particularly for efforts like DIB, which focus on the strategic level of cooperation and have many stakeholders within and outside DoD. AFRICOM's approval of country cooperation plans (CCPs) and staging of a Theater Synchronization Conference in 2014 were important steps in this process. In many ways, however, these efforts are just a starting point as security cooperation planning is an iterative process that requires regular and systematic coordination. Finally, as we discuss in the next section, AFRICOM faced even greater challenges assessing security cooperation, and DIB in particular.

What Will African Partners Accept?

While we did not interview African officials, the question of what African partners will accept helped identify some of the greatest challenges to effective DIB implementation. Both DoD and AFRICOM staff expressed strong views about the challenges in understanding the interests of African partners. In some cases, such as Liberia, funds were budgeted but not used because African officials did not identify productive ways to spend the money. In other cases, DoD officials argued that many African partners did not want DIB assistance.[6] National pride and suspicion of U.S. intentions created obstacles for many potential DIB activities. While this is certainly true in some cases, Africa is not unique in this regard. For example, DoD's Southern Command faces similar challenges in parts of Latin America, yet has a relatively robust and effective DIB program.[7]

Helping a partner country reform its institutions can be a particularly sensitive topic, because these efforts can touch on issues of national sovereignty more than, say, training an army battalion. Thus, those planning and implementing DIB must be especially clear about their guidance and well prepared for their mission. Implementers must have both relevant substantive expertise and strong relationship-building skills that are attuned to the region. For example, officials pointed out that lessons many U.S. implementers learned in Iraq and Afghanistan can be counterproductive in Africa.[8]

Based on our interviews and our review of DIB-related documents, those most responsible for engaging with partner officials appeared to have insufficient preparation and guidance for explaining DIB opportunities to African officials and for tying DIB to other U.S. and African country goals. The full range of DIB options and how they connected to other security cooperation efforts were not always clear to

---

[6]   Interviews with DoD officials, April and July 2014.

[7]   See Perry et al., forthcoming.

[8]   Interviews with DoD officials, April 2014.

both African partners and the Americans trying to explain it. Far more than high-level guidance, those working with African partners need simple, plainly worded information and training to help them communicate the relative advantages of various DIB opportunities.

Identifying DIB Programs Applicable to Africa

Given the challenges laid out above, it is important to identify programs for Africa that can support DIB goals, that link to broader U.S. policy goals, and that DoD can carry out successfully. Therefore, we developed a database of programs that DoD could use to identify candidate programs. Such a database does not solve all the problems of selecting DIB programs, but it provides a good starting point. Additional steps, such as tailoring the programs to specific countries and coordinating them with host nation officials, would be necessary to arrive at a finalized list of DIB programs for implementation.

Purpose of a DIB Programs Database

U.S. security cooperation activities involve a variety of programs and authorities that make it difficult even for security cooperation planners to have a clear view of all existing instruments at their disposal and to have a clear picture of the full spectrum of security cooperation programs active in a country at any one time. The Defense Institute of Security Assistance Management's list of security cooperation programs, for instance, contains 90 such mechanisms.[9] The *Army Security Cooperation Handbook*, which only includes mechanisms of relevance to the Army, has 53 of them.[10] A 2013 RAND report lists a staggering 165 security cooperation mechanisms.[11]

A comprehensive database of DIB-related programs that synopsized activities, purpose, and geographic scope could highlight oppor-

---

[9] Defense Institute of Security Assistance Management, *Security Cooperation Programs Through Fiscal Year 2014*, Revision 14.2, undated.

[10] U.S. Department of the Army, 2013b.

[11] Moroney, Thaler, and Hogler, 2013.

tunities from programs that one might not immediately associate with DIB; identify gaps, such as U.S. objectives that may be inadequately covered by existing programs; and detect duplication and inefficiencies among existing programs. The following section describes such a database and details the process through which it was built.

Methodology

The methodology used to build the RAND database of DIB-related programs relevant for Africa is similar to the one used to build RAND's global DIB database.[12] We searched for DIB-labeled programs in the above-mentioned *Army Security Cooperation Handbook* and 2013 RAND report on security cooperation mechanisms used by combatant commands. These two documents specifically flagged DIB as one of their "purpose" categories. We then employed a six-step process to develop the database.

In **step one**, we selected all mechanisms with DIB listed as one of their purposes. After removing mechanisms that are no longer active, we were left with 69 mechanisms identified as DIB.[13]

In **step two**, we asked subject-matter experts whether they could identify any glaring omission in the resulting list of mechanisms, including some too recent to have been included in either publication. Eight more mechanisms were identified, raising the total to 78.

Step three consisted of sorting these mechanisms into three categories: programs, authorities, and funds. A *program* is a set of activities or events, or the institution carrying out these sets of activities or events; an *authority* is the specific approval source to use certain funds for certain purposes; and a *fund* is a source of money set aside for a specific purpose. Here, we focus on programs to highlight the events and activities that get implemented in partner nations, rather than the mechanisms (or financial resources) that allow such events and activi-

---

[12] See Perry et al., forthcoming.

[13] In some instances, mechanisms were nested in each other. For instance, the Defense Education Enhancement Program (DEEP) is a part of the Wales Initiative Fund (WIF). We also removed from the database three programs that had expired or were never funded, as well as multinational military centers of excellence, which is more of a NATO than U.S. program.

ties to take place. Out of the 78 security cooperation mechanisms, we found 70 programs, four authorities, and four funds, for which we outlined activities and purposes, as well as geographic focus.

Step four ensured that all the programs outlined in the database matched the definition of DIB as outlined in the draft DoD Directive discussed in Chapter Two. DIB programs are considered as such based on the type of actor they engaged (the political and strategic level of defense institutions, rather than operational units) and the type of activities they performed (e.g., promoting democratic civilian control of armed forces, improving systems for effective functioning of defense governance).[14] A total of 20 programs (out of 70) did not fit this definition, leaving 50 actual DIB programs in the database.

Step five removed from the database all programs that are not relevant for Africa, based on their geographic focus. This left 47 Africa-relevant DIB programs.

The **sixth and final step** consisted of categorizing these 47 Africa-relevant DIB programs into one of three types, based on their focus and activities:[15]

- Type 1 programs ("defense familiarization") are of two kinds: Type 1a programs aim to familiarize partner nations with DIB best practices through episodic engagements, such as exercises, seminars, or information exchanges (12 programs); Type 1b programs consist of prolonged engagements, such as the deployment of liaison officers or personnel exchanges (four programs).
- Type 2 programs ("defense professionalization") include education and training activities, conferences, seminars, and workshops (22 programs).

---

[14] Under Secretary of Defense for Policy, 2015.

[15] When a program could be categorized in more than one type, we assigned it the highest possible one. For instance, WIF-DIB activities include ministry-to-ministry engagement (Type 3), PME (Type 2), and high-level meetings (Type 1). Consequently, it is presented in the database as a Type 3 program.

- Type 3 programs ("defense management") include ministerial advisors and engagement, and creation or support to new institutions (nine programs).

These three types of programs have different uses. Partner nations with mature defense institutions value Type 1 programs to exchange best practices. New partners benefit from the "lighter" engagement Type 1 programs can offer before more-substantial reform can be planned. The large-scale SSR undertaken in post-conflict settings, as discussed earlier, is mostly conducted with Type 2 and 3 activities—as are any in-depth DIB-related interactions conducted around the world.

Results and Implications

The resulting Africa-relevant DIB programs show the bulk of activities in the defense professionalization (Type 2) programs, with fewer programs in the defense management and the defense familiarization categories (see Table 3.2). The lowest number of programs is in the category that includes the most-intensive and focused types of engagement, which is the defense management category (Type 3 programs).

Type 3 Programs: Defense Management

Table 3.3 provides the types of activities and objectives of the nine defense management (Type 3) programs we identified for Africa. We characterize five of these programs as DIB-focused and four as programs that could directly support DIB.

In Africa, DIRI is the flagship program for DIB—DSCA describes it as "DoD's primary security cooperation tool for support-

Table 3.2
Number of Global and Africa-Relevant DIB Programs According to Type of Activities

Type of DIB Programs	Number of DIB Programs	Number of Africa-Relevant DIB Programs
Type 1: "defense familiarization"	16	16
Type 2: "defense professionalization"	25	22
Type 3: "defense management"	9	9

Table 3.3
Africa-Relevant Defense Management (Type 3) Programs

Type of program		Program Name	Type of Activities	Intended Outcome
DIB-focused programs	1.	Defense Institutional Reform Initiative (DIRI)	Conduct organizational assessments and establish a roadmap to address issues identified	Improve systems for effective functioning of defense governance and execution of activities
	2.	Wales (formerly Warsaw) Initiative Fund–DIB (WIF-DIB)	Assess partner nation's defense institutions, develop education activities, military-to-military engagement to address organizational gaps	Assess and address institutional and organizational gaps in partner nation
	3.	Defense Institute of International Legal Studies (DIILS)	Resident and mobile courses on legal matters for foreign military officers, legal advisors, and related civilians; assistance in setting up or reforming military justice systems, as well as improving accountability and transparency of legal systems	Professionalize defense personnel, both civilian and military, in legal matters; establish or improve national-level justice defense institutions
	4.	Ministry of Defense Advisors Program (MoDA)	Deployment of senior DoD civilian employees to advise foreign officials from ministries involved with national security	Improve systems for effective functioning of defense governance and execution of activities
	5.	Security Governance Initiative (SGI)	Assess partner nations' security sector with a focus on processes and institutions, develop strategies and programs to address institutional gaps, and regular monitoring and adjustment (when needed) of these programs	Improve partner nations' ability to provide security to their citizens, mitigate risks of instability and radicalization

Table 3.3—Continued

Type of program	Program Name	Type of Activities	Intended Outcome
Additional programs that could directly support DIB	1. Center for Army Lessons Learned (CALL) International Engagements	Lessons-learned seminars, courses, and briefings; assistance to partner nations in setting up their own lessons-learned centers	Create or improve institutional capability to identify, archive, and retrieve lessons learned
	2. State Partnership Program (SPP)	Partnering of U.S. states with other nations in support of combatant command objectives. Activities vary according to partnership	Intended outcomes vary according to partnership; may include professionalizing defense personnel and establishing or improving defense institutions
	3. Defense Education Enhancement Program (DEEP)	Peer-to-peer mentoring, curriculum revision, and workshops for PME institutions	Reform and expand the PME capacity of NATO PfP countries and members of other select NATO partnerships
	4. African Military Education Program (AMEP)	Peer-to-peer mentoring, curriculum revision, and workshops for PME institutions	Reform and expand the PME capacity of Sub-Saharan African countries

NOTE: Types 1 and 2 are discussed later in the chapter.

ing partner nation efforts to develop accountable, effective and efficient defense governance institutions."[16]

AFRICOM is one of the three regional combatant commands set as priorities for DIRI engagement in FY 2015.[17] DIRI was authorized in 2009, began operations in early 2010, and has since been offering ministry-to-ministry engagement whereby subject-matter experts conduct organizational assessments of partner nations and establish a roadmap with them to address problematic areas.[18] The program focuses on the four key processes that form the foundation of defense institutions: the partner nation's defense strategy and policy; its defense resource management; its logistics; and its human resources management.[19] As of mid-2014, DIRI had undertaken engagements in several African countries (shown in Table 3.4), including Guinea, Liberia, the Democratic Republic of the Congo (DRC), South Sudan, and Libya, although efforts in South Sudan and Libya have been impeded by internal insecurity and political instability.[20]

WIF used to be an important DIB program not available in Africa, because its funding source limited it to the European and Central Asian countries of the PfP. Since the September 2014 NATO

Table 3.4
DIRI Country Engagements FYs 2012–2014

	FY 2012	FY 2013	FY 2014
Countries	DRC Liberia Libya Guinea	DRC Liberia Guinea	DRC Libya Guinea Botswana
Number of countries	4	3	4

SOURCE: Discussion with DIRI representative, August 2014.

---

[16] DSCA, *Fiscal Year 2014 Budget Estimates*, April 2013, p. 474.

[17] The other two being Pacific Command and Central Command. See DSCA, *Fiscal Year 2015 Budget Estimates*, March 2014, p. 486.

[18] DSCA, *Fiscal Year 2012 Budget Estimates*, February 2011, pp. 431 and 470.

[19] DIRI, "Building Defense Institutional Capacity," briefing, September 2013.

[20] DSCA, 2011, p. 440; DSCA, 2013, pp. 515–516; and DSCA, 2014, pp. 483 and 485.

Wales Summit, however, WIF has opened to other NATO partners, including members of the Mediterranean Dialogue.[21] As of early 2015, this meant that five African countries could become WIF recipients: Algeria, Egypt, Mauritania, Morocco, and Tunisia. This opening of WIF to Northern African countries may complement the work done by the Security Governance Initiative (SGI) in West and East Africa, with some overlap in Tunisia.

DIILS offers resident and mobile courses on legal matters to foreign military officers, legal advisors, and related civilians. The only reason DIILS is mentioned here as a defense management (Type 3) program is because it also assists partner nations in setting up or reforming their military justice systems and improving the accountability and transparency of their legal systems, which makes it more than an education and training program. DIILS has undertaken a number of activities on the African continent. The institute's largest single African engagement has been in the DRC, when it reviewed issues ranging from command responsibility to gender-based violence with more than 1,600 new recruits of the Armed Forces of the Democratic Republic of the Congo over the course of four days.[22] DIILS has been carrying out resident and mobile courses in many more African countries, including (as of FY 2012) Morocco, Tunisia, Côte d'Ivoire, Namibia, Ethiopia, Kenya, Tanzania, Mozambique, Burkina Faso, Ghana, Malawi, Mauritania, Mali, Guinea, Chad, Djibouti, Nigeria, South Sudan, Uganda, Gabon, DRC, Rwanda, Burundi, and Botswana.[23] Table 3.5 lists these engagements.

MoDA deploys senior DoD civilian employees to advise officials of partner nations' ministries of defense and interior, as well as other ministries involved with national security. The program embeds DoD experts in partner security institutions based on requirements identified by partner nations (e.g., planning, logistics, financial management, personnel, and readiness). Although MoDA was not yet present in

---

[21] DSCA, *Fiscal Year 2016 Budget Estimates*, February 2015, pp. 418–419.

[22] DIILS, "In Congo (DRC) DILLS Conducts Its Largest Seminar," web page, March 12, 2014.

[23] DIILS, *Annual Report Fiscal Year 2012*, Newport, R.I., 2013.

Table 3.5
DIILS Country Engagement, by Fiscal Year

	FY 2012[a]	FY 2013	FY 2014
Countries	Botswana	DRC	Botswana
	Burkina Faso	Botswana	Burkina Faso
	Burundi	Burundi	Burundi
	Chad	Côte d'Ivoire	Chad
	Côte d'Ivoire	Djibouti	Comoros
	Djibouti	Guinea	Côte d'Ivoire
	DRC	Kenya	DRC
	Ethiopia	Liberia	Ghana
	Gabon	Mauritania	Kenya
	Ghana	Niger	Mali
	Guinea	Tunisia	Mauritania
	Kenya	Uganda	Morocco
	Malawi		Niger
	Mali		Nigeria
	Mauritania		Uganda
	Morocco		
	Mozambique		
	Namibia		
	Nigeria		
	Rwanda		
	South Sudan		
	Tanzania		
	Tunisia		
	Uganda		
Number of countries	24	12	15

SOURCE: Discussion with DIILS representative, November 2014.
[a] The courses included both resident and mobile courses (DIILS, 2013).

Africa as of mid-2014 (Afghanistan, Kosovo, and Montenegro were the first three countries with MoDA advisors), three of the 16 countries nominated as candidates for potential MoDA deployment in FY 2013 were in Africa (Botswana, DRC, and Guinea).[24]

The most recent program is the SGI, which was announced by the White House at the close of the U.S.-Africa Leader's Summit—the first such summit to be organized by the U.S. government—on August 6, 2014. The SGI was created to further develop the "comprehensive approach to improving security sector governance and capacity to

---

[24] FY 2013 MoDA Annual Report, provided via email exchange with MoDA official, April 29, 2014.

address threats."[25] This initiative is reminiscent of the work that DIRI does, because it involves assessing partner nations' security institutions, identifying key gaps, and planning strategies—jointly with the partner nation—to fill these gaps. The SGI differs from DIRI, however, in that it is not limited to the defense sector but also includes such issues as policing or access to justice. The SGI also includes regular monitoring and evaluation of the programs put in place to address institutional gaps, so that these programs can be adjusted if needs change over time. It is also worth noting that, because it came as a result of the Africa summit, only African countries seem eligible, at this point, to be part of SGI, even though nothing in the description of the program seems to preclude it from being expanded to other regions in the future. The first six SGI recipients are Ghana, Kenya, Mali, Niger, Nigeria, and Tunisia. They were chosen, according to the White House, because each "has demonstrated partnership with the United States, expressed a desire to strengthen its security sector, and committed to the core elements of the initiative."[26]

The database also highlights four programs that may have the capacity to conduct DIB activities either directly or indirectly.

The Center for Army Lessons Learned International Engagements, at Fort Leavenworth, Kansas, conducts lessons-learned seminars, courses, and briefings within the United States and elsewhere as requested by DoD agencies or combatant commands. The center may play a role in building new defense institutions through one of its lesser-known activities, which is to assist partner nations in setting up their own lessons-learned centers as requested by U.S. Department of the Army Headquarters or the Training and Doctrine Command.[27] Arguably, this capacity—which is not a Center for Army Lessons Learned primary mission, but could be enhanced in the future for DIB purposes—would be of use mostly in mature armies whose basic functions, from staffing to budgeting and planning, can be judged satis-

---

[25] The White House, "Fact Sheet: Security Governance Initiative," web page, August 6, 2014.

[26] The White House, 2014.

[27] U.S. Department of the Army, 2013b, p. 23.

factory. In Africa, this capacity may, for example, be of use to defense forces in Morocco or South Africa, as well as at the supranational level, helping the AU strengthen its "lessons learned" capacity for its peace-keeping operations. In the future, such a capability could also be useful for the African Standby Force, either at the continental level or within each of the Force's regional brigades.[28]

The State Partnership Program (SPP) contains as many different types of initiatives as there are partnerships between U.S. states and partner nations.[29] The potential relevance of SPP for Africa has been limited to date because of the small number of partnerships with African countries, but could grow, particularly as the Army implements its Regionally Aligned Forces concept. As of July 2015, there were 70 state partnerships involving 76 countries, only 12 of which were in Africa (Benin, Botswana, Djibouti, Ghana, Kenya, Liberia, Morocco, Nigeria, Senegal, South Africa, Togo, and Tunisia).[30] All have armed forces that are relatively mature or have undergone major reforms in the past two decades (see Table 3.6).

DEEP aims to reform and expand the PME capacity of NATO PfP countries, with a focus on curriculum and faculty development. Its activities include peer-to-peer mentoring of partner nation faculty, curriculum revision, and workshops and courses on teaching methods. Although their focus on education would logically make them Type 2 programs, DEEP and AMEP are included in Type 3 programs because they affect partner nation defense education institutions as a whole rather than simply affecting some of the individuals working for these institutions.[31] DEEP is run by DoD (through OSD

---

[28] African Union Peace and Security, "The African Standby Force (ASF)," web page, updated April 19, 2015.

[29] Lawrence Kapp and Nina M. Serafino, *The National Guard State Partnership Program: Background, Issues, and Options for Congress*, Washington, D.C.: Congressional Research Service, RL41957, August 15, 2011, p. 5.

[30] National Guard, "State Partnership Program," web page, undated; National Guard, State Partnership Program map, July 1, 2015.

[31] Partnership for Peace Consortium of Defense Academies and Security Studies Institutes, "Defense Education Enhancement Program," web page, undated.

Table 3.6
U.S. States and African Partner Nation

U.S. State/National Guard	African Country Partner
California	Nigeria
Kentucky	Djibouti
Massachusetts	Kenya
Michigan	Liberia
New York	South Africa
North Carolina	Botswana
North Dakota	Benin, Ghana, Togo
Utah	Morocco
Vermont	Senegal
Wyoming	Tunisia

SOURCE: National Guard, 2015.

Policy) in conjunction with NATO. The PfP Consortium, through DoD's Marshall Center, is its executive agent. Although primarily designed for NATO PfP countries, DEEP has been extended on one occasion to an African country, Mauritania, which benefited from DEEP through its membership in NATO's Mediterranean Dialogue.[32] This suggests that the program could be expanded to the four other African members of the Dialogue: Algeria, Morocco, Tunisia, and Egypt.

Sub-Saharan Africa has its own equivalent of the DEEP program, at least in terms of activities and mission: AMEP, initiated by the U.S. Congress in 2012 to improve PME in Africa.[33] The program

---

[32] Jean d'Andurain and Alan Stolberg, "Defense Education Enhancement Program: The NATO Functional Clearing-House on Defense Education," *Connections: The Quarterly Journal*, Vol. 11, No. 4, Fall 2012, p. 54.

[33] DIILS, too, provides curriculum development to defense institutions, but exclusively on legal topics. For instance, DIILS was tasked by OSD in 2008 to develop a curriculum for human rights and international humanitarian law training for the DRC Armed Forces (Ste-

is run by the State Department, but its executive agent is DoD's Africa Center for Security Studies. AMEP's purpose is similar to DEEP's and includes the same types of activities. As of mid-2014, AMEP had engaged or was set on engaging 13 countries: Botswana, Ethiopia, Malawi, Mozambique, Niger, Nigeria, Zambia, Ghana, Burundi, Chad, Kenya, Uganda, and Gabon.[34] Table 3.7 lists countries engaged in 2013, 2014, and 2015. Table 3.8 outlines the main similarities and differences between DEEP and AMEP.

Type 2 Programs: Defense Professionalization

Beyond the defense management (Type 3) programs, the database highlights 22 education or training programs (Type 2) that do some degree of DIB (see Table 3.9). The topics covered range from educating defense officials on counterterrorism at the strategic level (Combating Terrorism Fellowship Program) to ensuring that institutions have the capacity to properly manage their resources (Defense Resource Man-

Table 3.7
Africa Military Education Program Country Engagements, FYs 2013–2015

	FY 2013	FY 2014	FY 2015
Countries	Botswana Chad Ethiopia Malawi Mozambique Niger Nigeria	Burundi Chad Gabon Ghana Kenya Nigeria Uganda Zambia	Burkina Faso Burundi Cameroon Djibouti Ghana Madagascar Niger Rwanda South Africa Tanzania
Number of countries	7	8	10

SOURCE: Department of Defense Internal Interviews.
NOTE: FY 2013–2015 funding has ranged from $75,000 to $400,000, depending on program.

---

phen Rosenlund, "DIILS at 20 Years—Advancing the Rule of Law Worldwide," *JAG Magazine*, 2012, p. 20).

[34] Phone interview with DEEP and AMEP representatives, August 2014.

Table 3.8
Comparison of DEEP and AMEP

	DEEP	AMEP
Region	NATO PfP partners (Europe and Eurasia) with exceptions	Sub-Saharan Africa
Oversight authority	NATO/DoD	State Department
Executive agent	PfP Consortium at the Marshall Center	Africa Center for Security Studies
Implementers	U.S./international subject-matter experts on curriculum and faculty development	U.S. subject-matter experts on curriculum and faculty development
Activities	Support for curriculum and faculty development in partner nations' defense education institutions	Support for curriculum and faculty development in partner nations' defense education institutions
Approach	Demand-driven	Demand-driven

SOURCES: Phone interviews with DEEP and AMEP representatives, August and September 2014.

Table 3.9
Africa-Relevant Defense Professionalization (Type 2) Programs

Program Name	Program Description
General education	
Center for Civil-Military Relations	Courses, workshops, visits, seminars, research and publications, exercises, and distance learning, all focusing on promoting good civil-military relations, supporting DIB, supporting peacebuilding, and combating violent extremism.
Distribution to Certain Personnel of Education and Training Materials and Information Technology to Enhance Military Interoperability with the Armed Forces	Education and training of foreign military and civilian personnel through electronic educational material to improve interoperability.
Foreign military sales (training and advice component)	Sales of defense articles and services (including training) from the U.S. government to foreign governments.
Foreign officers admission to the Naval Postgraduate School	Advanced education for active-duty military officers or civilian government employees of partner nations.

Table 3.9—Continued

Program Name	Program Description
Foreign participation in the Senior Reserve Officers' Training Corps	Participation of foreign students in basic course, basic camp, or advanced course.
Foreign service academy semester abroad exchanges	Participation of up to 24 students from the U.S. Military Academy, Naval Academy, and Air Force Academy in an exchange with cadets from foreign military academies to spend a semester abroad.
Foreign student attendance at the service academies	Four-year fellowship for a foreigner to attend service academies.
International Military Education and Training	Grant military education and training for foreign military and defense-related civilian personnel.
Professional military education exchanges	Attendance of foreign military personnel at U.S. professional military education institutions (other than service academies).
Regional centers for security studies	DoD institutions studying security issues relating to a specific region of the world, involving military and civilian participants and acting as forums for research and exchange of ideas.
Sergeants Major Academy International Fellows Program	Foreign equivalents of master sergeants and sergeant majors attend the Sergeants Major Academy courses with their U.S. counterparts to prepare for positions of responsibility within their defense and military institutions.
U.S. Army Security Cooperation Training Teams	Army or joint training and technical assistance teams deployed to partner nations in support of foreign military sales cases, providing advice, training, and support on equipment, technology, doctrine, tactics, and weapon systems.
Niche expertise	
Assignments to Improve Education and Training in Information Security	Temporary assignment of a member of a foreign military force to DoD to learn about information security threats, management, and response.
Civil-military emergency preparedness	Assists partner countries or regions in increasing their civil and military disaster preparedness capabilities.
Combating Terrorism Fellowship Program	Education and training events aimed at mid- and senior-level foreign defense and security officials, to increase counterterrorism capabilities and build a global network of counterterrorism experts.
Defense Resource Management Institute	Resident and mobile courses on effective allocation of resources in defense organizations.

Table 3.9—Continued

Program Name	Program Description
Foreign participation in the Uniformed Services University of the Health Sciences	Attendance to one of the three schools for military officers at the Uniformed Services University of the Health Sciences.
International Defense Acquisition Resource Management (IDARM)	Defense acquisition courses for foreign military officers and senior civilian officials.
Research	
DoD Senior Military College International Student Program	Provides opportunities for senior foreign military officers to conduct study and research on security-related topics.
U.S. Army Center of Military History Intern Program	Internship for one or more officer or cadet who receives mentoring and is allocated a workspace at the Center for Military History.
Cultural activities/education	
Field studies program for international military and civilian students and military-sponsored visitors	Familiarizes international military students with U.S. values, history, and way of life.
Service academy foreign and cultural exchange activities	Cultural immersion experience for U.S. Military Academy and foreign cadets.

agement Institute). ACSS and NESA play an important role in providing PME to African countries, including its DIB component (see our case study on DoD regional centers in Appendix B). Type 2 programs help provide the educational foundation crucial to strengthening transparent and accountable defense institutions.

Type 1 Programs: Defense Familiarization
Finally, the database includes 16 defense familiarization (Type 1) programs, which include both episodic engagements (Type 1a) and more-prolonged engagement (Type 1b):

- Type 1a programs:
  - High-level talks programs: African Land Forces Summit, Army-to-Army Staff Talks, Operator Engagement Talks, U.S. Army TRADOC Training and Doctrine Conferences

- High-level visits programs: Distinguished Visitors Orientation Tours and Orientation Tours, Service Chief Counterpart Visit Program, U.S. Army Distinguished Foreign Visits, U.S. Army International Visitors Program
- Information exchange programs: Imagery Intelligence and Geospatial Information, Transfer of Technical Data
- Research cooperation programs: Global Research Watch Program, U.S. Army Center of Military History International History Program.
- Type 1b programs:
  - Liaisons or personnel exchange programs: Defense Personnel Exchange Program, the Foreign Liaison Officer Program, non-reciprocal exchange of defense personnel
  - Attendance of U.S. officers to foreign military staff or senior service colleges: School of Other Nations program.

Overall, this database highlights the diversity of DIB programs that apply to Africa. These programs cover every type of possible activity, from information exchange and contacts, at the lowest level, to the sending of embedded advisors who can directly help partner nations reshape their institutions toward more efficiency and accountability. There are especially promising DIB opportunities in the area of education, with 22 relevant programs available for African partners. Some of the programs highlighted in this database are not generally perceived as doing DIB, but can be steered in that direction given the appropriate guidance and incentives. Doing more DIB, therefore, does not necessarily require creating new programs, but may also be done through a better focusing of those already in existence—for instance, through the addition of new state partnerships or by leveraging the DoD regional center focusing on Africa.

Africa also has some unique programs—for example, SGI, which represents an important new DIB effort; and the African Land Forces Summit, which consists of a biennial conference gathering senior land forces officers from the United States and African countries with the purpose of building relationships, improving defense cooperation, and exchanging information. Some programs that were initially not applicable to Africa, such as WIF-DIB, now have the potential to be implemented in some African countries, further broadening the range of security cooperation tools available to the United States to assist partner nations in building their defense institutions. While navigating such a large and varied array of programs can be challenging, it provides options for implementing DIB in ways that may be more palatable to sensitive partners—for example, offering an exchange of personnel to a partner nation reluctant to host a U.S. advisor.

What Types of Programs for What Types of Partner?

Security cooperation projects, including DIB, are initially prioritized at the annual AFRICOM Theater Synchronization Conference held in September. This and several other workshops and various informal meetings are part of the CCP resourcing process that starts in January and ends in December with final funding decisions.[35] Participants in these gatherings include country team representatives, country desk officers, the AFRICOM Strategy, Plans, and Programs Division (J5) staff, and other stakeholders.

However, in all of this, there does not appear to be an established set of criteria that might be used to help prioritize candidate security cooperation—and especially DIB—projects. Instead, prioritization is often ad hoc and based on informal sharing of opinions more than analysis. Several stakeholders expressed significant concerns about this, and more generally about problems coordinating DIB activities. One official stated that "[selection and prioritization] is broken in the system. . . . The command can't agree where to ask for [DIB] efforts to be applied."[36] OSD staff, in frustration, obtained nominations from its own country desk officers and contacted U.S. embassy officials directly—AFRICOM was cut out of the loop.[37] AFRICOM appointed a DIB coordinator in 2014 with experience in other commands, reflecting a recognition that the DIB project prioritization process needs improvement.

---

[35] Charles W. Hooper, "United States Africa Command: Theater Synchronization," briefing, AFRICOM Strategy, Plans, and Programs (J5), June 7, 2013.

[36] Interviews with OSD and AFRICOM staff, Summer 2014.

[37] Interviews with OSD and AFRICOM staff, Summer 2014.

Like Central Command, AFRICOM has established lines of effort (LOEs), but security cooperation is not one of them. Instead, it is a component of all six LOEs—i.e., it cuts across all of them. This makes it more difficult to establish criteria for selecting and prioritizing countries and DIB projects that might help achieve security cooperation goals. Instead, AFRICOM expands the ten security cooperation focus areas from the *Guidance for Employment of the Force* (not publicly available) into numerous AFRICOM focus areas. Several do indeed focus on DIB such as human resource management and logistics and infrastructure management.

DIB Program Activity Synchronization

AFRICOM actively sought to synchronize steady-state activities through three essential elements: a synchronized framework, standardized processes, and a web-based dashboard.[38] AFRICOM's steady state activities were designed to satisfy theater end-states along several LOEs.[39] In AFRICOM's 2012 theater campaign plan (TCP), five of the six LOEs were operationally focused and not captured by OSD's definition of DIB.[40] The sixth LOE was "strengthening defense capabilities."[41] The 2016 TCP did not include a specific DIB LOE.

AFRICOM used a "Synchronization Board" made up of planners from across the command to consolidate activity planning. It consists of eight working groups: Regional Synchronization; Operations;

---

[38] Hooper, 2013, slide 4.

[39] Hooper, 2013, slide 6.

[40] In late 2015, AFRICOM released an updated TCP (2016–2020) that made substantial changes to how DIB is assessed and conducted within AFRICOM's area of responsibility. According to the 2016 TCP, DIB is a "key task" supported through security force assistance at the executive direction, generating force, and operating force levels. AFRICOM LOEs have also been realigned to achieve operational aspects of theater end-states. Finally, each new LOE has an associated intermediate military objective (IMO) that helps to create a baseline assessment of partner nation capability, and monitor partner nation progress. Commander, U.S. Africa Command, *AFRICOM Theater Campaign Plan 2000-16, Fiscal Years 2016-2020*, August 2015. Not available to the general public.

[41] Incidentally, this LOE appeared to be prioritized last within AFRICOM's area of responsibility.

Joint Command and Control; Consolidated Health; Theater Synchronization; Joint Exercise; Security Cooperation; and Women, Peace, & Security.[42] The Synchronization Board retained the sole authority to approve changes to the focus areas. Activities and resource allocation come when CCPs are finalized—or as part of the State Department's integrated country strategies (ICSs).[43]

Prospects for Expanding the Scope of DIB Programs in Africa

Although numerous programs that engage in DIB or have the potential to do so are already present in Africa, in some cases their presence remains limited in spite of considerable need on the part of the United States' African partners. In some cases, this occurs because programs are still new. As of early 2015, MoDA was only in the process of becoming global, and it may take several years before this program, if successful, establishes a solid presence in Africa. SGI, too, is in its first year of activity and it is probably too early to tell whether it will be deemed sufficiently successful to be expanded to additional countries in the future. SGI represented, in some ways, an extension of the DIRI program to African priority countries, since both programs present a number of similar features, including defense and security sector assessments, the identification of key gaps, and the planning of strategies to address these gaps.

One of the most promising ways to further promotion of DIB in Africa could be through the development of more state partnerships than the 12 that currently exist on the continent. The SPP looks at establishing longer-term relations with partner nations than any other DIB program currently in existence. The nature of the work done by the National Guard (for instance, its expertise in disaster response) also makes it particularly apt at navigating the civil-military divide in partner nations and engaging diverse security actors. The National Guard also develops deep knowledge of the partner country, ranging from local political dynamics to which roads on a map actually exist. As a member of the Michigan National Guard—partnered with Latvia and

---

[42] Hooper, 2013, slide 16.

[43] Hooper, 2013, slide 19.

Liberia—noted, "The Michigan National Guard *is* the legacy mission. We are there for decades."[44]

Overall, most programs with a DIB component are not region-specific and can be implemented in Africa. The few that are not are listed in Table 3.10. They include the Army Cyber Command Security Engagement, which builds cyber capabilities and has been limited to a small circle of U.S. allies. The Inter-American Air Forces Academy and the Western Hemisphere Institute for Security Cooperation are not opened to students and trainees from Africa, Europe, or Asia, but the educational need they address can largely be fulfilled by other institutions that are open to African countries, such as the Center for Civil-Military Relations or the Africa Center for Security Studies. It is also worth noting that with SGI, Africa now has its own institution building program.

A Structured Approach to Partner Country Selection

The previous section aimed to assist policy planners in identifying DIB programs that could apply to Africa. In addition to identifying DIB programs, AFRICOM planners need to prioritize partner countries to work with. As our interviews highlighted, prioritization is often ad hoc and based on informal sharing of opinions more than analysis. As part of RAND's global DIB assessment, Walt Perry and colleagues found this informal approach to DIB partner country prioritization was consistent across combatant commands.[45] Rather than rely on subjective metrics that may reflect short-term political considerations, Perry and colleagues recommend a more objective selection process based on external factors to help decisionmakers evaluate a country for possible DIB investments.[46] They suggest selecting priority candidates based

---

[44] Michigan National Guard interview 20141016-001, October 16, 2014.

[45] See Perry et al., 2015.

[46] This process is based on earlier work by Jennifer D. P. Moroney, Joe Hogler, Lianne Kennedy-Boudali, and Stephanie Pezard, *Integrating the Full Range of Security Cooperation Programs into Air Force, Planning: An Analytic Primer*, Santa Monica, Calif.: RAND Cor-

Table 3.10
Programs with a DIB Component for Regions Other than Africa

Name	Activities and Purpose	Region/Country Focus
Army Cyber Command Security Engagement	Cyber-related training events and information sharing designed to build partner nation cyber capability, increase collective cyber security, and promote cyber interoperability between U.S. and partner nations.	GEF-designated critical and key partner countries/regions; Strategic Command/Cyber Command–designated partner countries/regions; and Headquarters, Department of the Army–designated partner countries/organizations. Only the United Kingdom, Canada, Australia, and New Zealand so far.
Inter-American Air Forces Academy	Courses including the International Squadron Officer School, as well as courses on intelligence and logistics. Also includes mobile training teams and subject-matter expert exchanges.	Central and South American countries
Western Hemisphere Institute for Security Cooperation	Education and training for foreign military, law enforcement, and civilian personnel. Includes a Command and General Staff Officer Course and a Noncommissioned Officer Professional-Development Course.	Western Hemisphere

SOURCES: U.S. Department of the Army, 2013, pp. 17 and 54; Inter-American Air Forces Academy, brochure, Lackland Air Force Base, Tex.: U.S. Air Force, undated.

on their need and ability to gain from DIB investment by consulting publicly available indices of country characteristics, such as rule of law, political stability, political transparency, democracy, respect for human rights, and economic development (the six exemplar indicators used in their report).

Even among developing countries, there is a wide range of characteristics. Countries that have relatively greater rule of law, respect for

---

poration, TR-974-AF, 2011. Perry et al.'s process is designed to prioritize countries globally. The first two steps, select treaty partners and alter the list of priority treaty partners as necessary, are not applicable in the African context.

human rights, stability, transparency, democracy, and economic development are generally better prepared to work with and absorb U.S. investments. Other RAND research has highlighted the increased impact of U.S. security cooperation associated with such countries.[47] For DIB partner countries that have weaker domestic institutions and capacity, AFRICOM planners need to identify DIB programs and program goals that match countries' underlying conditions and set expectations in keeping with the range of likely outcomes.

The metrics presented below build on the dimensions suggested in RAND's global DIB assessment, but use a readily available dataset developed specifically to track African governance (the Ibrahim Index of African Governance [IIAG]). These metrics provide information on partner nations' ability to absorb DIB programs, as well as a measure of the potential risks, and likelihood of success, of the DIB programs under consideration. Our approach is designed to provide a more objective, analytical basis to facilitate the consultative prioritization process for AFRICOM DIB program planning without adding to the workload of DIB program directors. While this process is not intended to replace current AFRICOM partner nation selection, it may offer a useful supplemental tool.

Ibrahim Index of African Governance

Identifying relevant, comparative cross-national data for use in empirically based assessments of political and economic outcomes across the African continent is a perennial problem for analysts and planners. The Mo Ibrahim Foundation, which was founded to address issues of governance in Africa and has focused on the need to build governance recommendations on empirical assessments, has developed the com-

---

[47] Stephen Watts, *Identifying and Mitigating Risks in Security Sector Assistance for Africa's Fragile States*, Santa Monica, Calif.: RAND Corporation, RR-808-A, 2015; Michael J. McNerney, Angela O'Mahony, Thomas Szayna, Derek Eaton, Caroline Baxter, Colin P. Clarke, et al., *Assessing Security Cooperation as a Preventive Tool*, Santa Monica, Calif.: RAND Corporation, RR-350-A, 2014.

posite IIAG, which combines more than 100 variables from more than 30 sources.[48]

What sets the IIAG apart from other composite indicators is its data team's recognition of and sensitivity to the constraints that exist in the data used. The team's research approach is transparent, and it is explicit about its treatment of missing data—as well as the impact of missing data and outliers on their indices.[49] The large number of data indicators and sources, along with the acknowledged level of correlation between the indicators, provides greater confidence that the composite index serves as a relatively good proxy for countries' overall level of governance. Although countries' overall level of governance may not capture the specifics of their defense institutions, we expect that it does serve as a rough proxy for countries' need and ability to gain from DIB investment.

Figure 3.1 displays the 2013 IIAG scores for all African countries, highlighting Northern and Western African countries in dark blue. To show the range in Northern and Western Africa geographically, Figure 3.2 displays the ranges of IIIAG scores overlaid on a map of the region. The data are presented on a 0–100 scale, with a score of 100 representing the highest governance score possible (Mauritius received a score of 81.7, the highest score in 2013) and a score of 0 representing the lowest governance score (Somalia received a score of 8.6, the lowest score in 2013). Figure 3.1 also includes an overlay of vertical bars that divide the governance index into thirds to provide planners with a starting point to help prioritize DIB programs. In considering whether and what type of DIB activities to undertake with partner

---

[48] Underlying data for the IIAG are from other well-known databases, such as the World Bank's Worldwide Governance Indicators, the Economist Intelligence Unit, United Nations' UNICEF and World Health Organization, and Freedom House.

The IIAG methodology defines governance as "the provision of the political, social and economic public goods and services that a citizen has the right to expect from his or her state, and that a state has the responsibility to deliver to its citizens. We are concerned with outputs and outcomes of policy, rather than declarations of intent and de jure statutes, though at times it is necessary to use measurements of the presence of laws." For further explanation of operational dimensions, see Mo Ibrahim Foundation, "2014 IIAG Methodology," 2014.

[49] Mo Ibrahim Foundation, 2014.

Figure 3.1
African Governance Scores

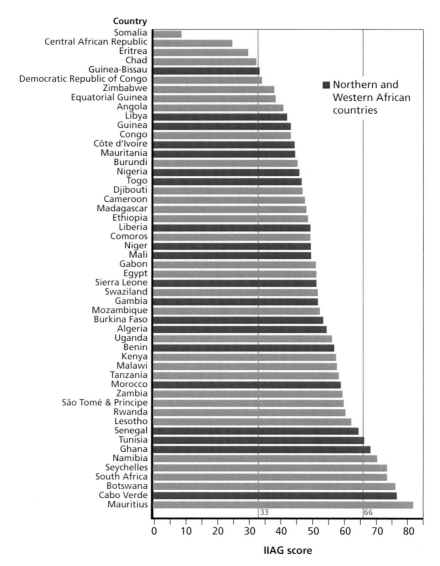

SOURCE: Mo Ibrahim Foundation, 2014.
RAND RR-1232-3.1

Figure 3.2
Map of Northern and Western African Governance Scores

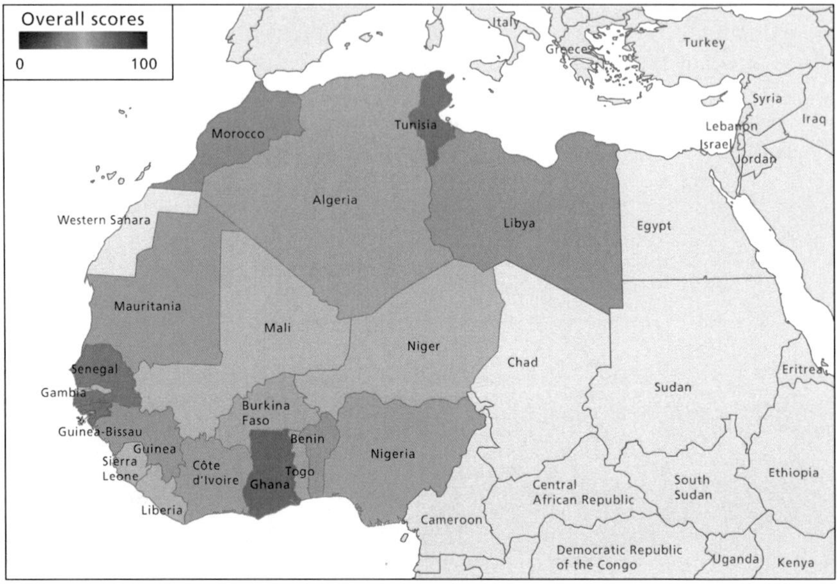

SOURCE: Mo Ibrahim Foundation, 2014, and RAND analysis.
RAND RR1232-3.2

countries, decisionmakers can see which countries have greater governance, which we expect is a broad proxy for their ability to absorb DIB assistance. For countries in the weakest third, decisionmakers and planners will need to consider carefully partner countries' absorptive capacity. For countries in the strongest third, partners may already have sufficiently strong defense institutions and may be candidates for different types of security cooperation. Table 3.11 shows this categorization and the recommendations by category. Examining the range of governance scores across Africa, most Northern and Western African countries fall within the middle third of governance scores, suggesting that they are good candidates for absorbing DIB investments. It is also notable that there is a wide range of governance captured within this group of countries.

The IIAG is composed of four main categories: safety and rule of law; participation and human rights; sustainable economic oppor-

Table 3.11
Risk Spectrum, by Country Category

Partner Nation Focus Area	Weakest Third (0–33)	Middle Third (34–66)	Strongest Third (67–100)
Assessment	Partner nation presents critical gaps in this governance area	Partner nation needs to improve its performance in this governance area	Partner nation may already be performing well in this governance area
Recommendation	The partner nation could use DIB assistance, but issues are so severe that it may prove difficult to use outside assistance effectively, making engagement risky	The partner nation can use DIB assistance to strengthen its performance in this area. DIB engagement may present risks, depending on how severe gaps are or where they are localized. A thorough needs assessment is required prior to engagement.	This area requires limited DIB support

SOURCE: RAND analysis.

tunity; and human development (see Table 3.12). Each of these four main categories are further sub-categorized, as shown in the right-hand column in Table 3.12. We expect these sub-categories can help planners to calibrate DIB programs to the needs and abilities of partner countries. In particular, we identified a subset of six IIAG indicators that we expect are especially relevant for helping planners to match DIB programs to partner country needs and abilities: rule of law, accountability, personal safety, national security, participation, and human rights. Table 3.13 presents Western African countries' scores for each of the six sub-categories.

As can be seen in Table 3.13, although most of the six sub-category scores are similar for each country, there are a few notable exceptions. For example, Benin has a lower-than-expected accountability score, which might highlight process concerns to emphasize in a DIB program. Alternatively, while most of Mauritania's domestic governance scores are relatively weak, its human rights score is higher than its other scores, suggesting an area of potential com-

Table 3.12
IIAG Governance Categories

Governance Category	Governance Sub-Category
Safety and Rule of Law	*Rule of law* *Accountability* *Personal safety* *National security*
Participation and Human Rights	*Political participation* *Human rights* Gender
Sustainable Economic Opportunity	Public management Business environment Infrastructure Rural sector
Human Development	Welfare Education Health

NOTE: The sub-categories in italics are the six sub-categories we focus on in our analysis.

petence to focus on in a DIB program. More broadly, the national security scores are substantially different from the other five more domestically oriented metrics. This category requires more contextual knowledge to interpret, as the results reflect both countries' exposure to external security threats and their own capacity to deter external threats.

Partner nations' scores in these different categories can help planners paint a picture of defense sector governance as a whole, and provide insights with regard to the areas most in need of assistance. Important to recognize, while these metrics are readily available and can be a useful input for informing planners about countries' broad-stroke strengths and weaknesses, they must be interpreted with caution. For example, the indicators used to measure national security (including cross-border tensions and government involvement in interstate conflict) may provide a misleading picture of some African countries. Also, because governance indices aggregate data collected in prior years, information can lag well behind current events. Nevertheless, in many

Table 3.13
IIAG Governance Categories: Scores by Country

	Rule of Law	Accountability	Personal Safety	National Security	Political Participation	Human Rights
Algeria	41	43	43	60	30	55
Benin	59	37	54	72	73	69
Burkina Faso	47	45	53	87	47	66
Cabo Verde	83	68	62	100	96	84
Côte d'Ivoire	27	29	38	73	52	46
Gambia	36	32	49	84	25	26
Ghana	85	57	54	83	80	78
Guinea	41	30	29	86	41	41
Guinea-Bissau	7	14	25	76	13	39
Liberia	42	37	45	82	65	48
Libya	13	18	26	76	53	38
Mali	39	44	50	62	44	54
Mauritania	38	27	31	77	29	47
Morocco	59	43	53	80	23	53
Niger	47	44	55	78	68	68
Nigeria	41	37	17	58	52	49
Senegal	70	48	61	75	75	75
Sierra Leone	55	41	55	83	61	64
Togo	49	37	48	85	36	53
Tunisia	56	57	44	80	62	59

SOURCE: Mo Ibrahim Foundation, 2014.

cases these metrics can stimulate a dialogue about country prioritization and what DIB activities may prove especially valuable.

Conclusion

- The data collected and categorized by the IIAG offers an additional source to help planners identify DIB programs applicable to specific African country needs.
- The IIAG data afford DIB planners two critical planning elements:
  - a structured approach to prioritizing partner country selection
  - a way to help planners match DIB programs to countries' needs and abilities, once partner countries are selected.
- Ultimately, integrating comparable, cross-national data into the DIB planning process can help DIB planners identify where activities may have the greatest effect in terms of current partner nation willingness and absorptive capacity to assist in developing effective security institutions.
- Using IIAG provides three key benefits:
  - The depiction of IIAG's aggregate data provides DIB planners an overview of country factors that can be included in the decision to engage or to wait until the atmosphere is ripe for intervention.[50]
  - Specific country-level drilldown data provided within the IIAG framework can expose additional elements for consideration when deciding whether to engage in DIB.
  - The IIAG data focus on factors specific to Africa—as such, rather than having a generalized or global database, the IIAG is tailored to the region. This allows for a more targeted approach in understanding current factors on the ground.

---

[50] One drawback of the IIAG is that it may not reflect current events on the ground. However, new IIAG statistics are released in tandem with the new fiscal year, which may aid in overall planning and budget cycles.

CHAPTER FOUR

Two Africa Case Studies

The two cases evaluated here—Liberia and Libya—represent the first type of DIB characterized in Chapter Two: large-scale, sweeping reforms that overhaul defense establishments and replace them with more efficient and accountable ones. Both experienced significant conflicts where institutions required a complete overhaul, and capacity-building efforts had transformational potential.[1] Yet this potential for high gains came with high risks, particularly in a country like Libya, where political and security gains have failed to take hold. As mentioned in Chapter Two, countries emerging from civil war or other conflicts tend to be more likely to accept major reforms; yet, their needs are immense and require large investments. The cases studied in this chapter presented challenging but illustrative examples for DIB. Liberia provided a case where the U.S. government has conducted DIB for many years. The successes and setbacks there effectively illustrate many of the lessons identified in our review of SSR literature and through our interviews with subject-matter experts. Although implementation was delayed due to insecurity, Libya provided a case that involved extensive DIB planning, both across the U.S. government and with multinational partners from 2012 to 2014, planning that built on at least some lessons from past efforts in other countries. Additional case studies reflecting different environments and levels of effort could help policymakers refine and expand on our conclusions.

---

[1] The other two types of DIB involve sending advisors to assist key defense officials or providing education and training to develop more professional defense personnel. See Chapter One.

While both Liberia and Libya present specialized cases, shared themes emerge between them. First, it is critical to have willing, capable, and engaged officials from partner countries. In both cases, understanding which actors had the authority, ability, and will to implement change was important. As in any country, there is considerable political wrangling among actors over what changes to make and how much to follow the guidance (or implicit coercion) of foreign actors. DIB planners need a nuanced understanding of national and organizational politics so they can identify and support willing and capable partners to participate and invest national resources into the effort. This finding echoes three of the principles of the *African Union Policy Framework on Security Sector Reform*: emphasizing national responsibility and national commitment; making sure there is a national vision for SSR (to guide external support); and making SSR context-specific.[2] In Liberia, there was great demand for U.S. support but little appetite for ownership and Liberian leadership commitment often wavered. In Libya, extreme instability and ongoing conflict severely undermined DIB and defense force training efforts. It is also imperative to match DIB ends to means. Overly ambitious goals risk overwhelming the partner country's absorptive capacity and risk creating fatigue on the DIB implementer's side. Expending time and money—or keeping resources on standby for a mission that does not happen—may eventually lead to disillusionment without at least incremental progress.[3]

Second, coordination remains a fundamental challenge within DoD, across the U.S. government, and with other stakeholders. While coordination was reportedly effective in some cases, it remained ad hoc and often personality driven in others. For instance, close personal contacts among DIRI, the State Department defense advisor, and the embassy country team, and contractors in Liberia helped to link a foreign military financing (FMF) case to a DIRI logistics project, incen-

---

[2]   African Union Commission, undated.

[3]   For a discussion on taking incremental steps through experimentation or "problem-driven learning," see Matt Andrews, *The Limits of Institutional Reform in Development: Changing Rules for Realistic Solutions*, New York: Cambridge University Press, January 2014.

tivizing Liberian buy-in and commitment to the project.[4] Conversely, weaker coordination between DIRI and the AFRICOM J5 led to duplicative planning efforts for a Liberian National Defense Strategy.[5] A focal point for future consideration is how to strengthen processes so that they survive personality clashes and staff rotations.

Third, a key process that needs strengthening is integration of DIB tools into AFRICOM planning. Although AFRICOM staff recognized the institutional requirements to sustain the capabilities they developed, security cooperation planning and activities in Liberia and Libya were primarily oriented toward tactical/operational level security force assistance. The cases highlighted the coordination challenges for DIB in particular, because of uncertainty about what constituted DIB, the role of DIRI (single DIB program or facilitator of DIB more generally?), and OSD and AFRICOM responsibilities for planning and implementation.

These shared themes are well known to DIB practitioners in the field. The objective here is to move from recognizing essential principles to identifying concrete ways for OSD and AFRICOM to navigate challenges and implement best practices. Although the spectrum of U.S. security sector assistance activities includes many programs and authorities, these case studies primarily focus on DoD's DIB tools and their integration into AFRICOM and embassy plans. For each case, we look at the history of DIB efforts, how planners developed their strategy and established objectives, harmonization across the U.S. government and beyond, how the partner nation was prioritized, how progress was assessed, and overall insights.

---

[4] DIRI interview 20141001-001, October 1, 2014; and email communication with country team official, January 2015.

[5] U.S. Africa Command, *Liberia Country Cooperation Plan*, undated a, and email communication with country team, State Department, and DIRI personnel, January 2015.

Liberia Case Study

DIB in Liberia began approximately ten years ago, when the United States agreed to take on the task of reconstituting Liberia's armed forces and Ministry of Defense (MoD). As mentioned, the U.S. DIB experience in Liberia is an example of the first type of DIB: post-conflict, complete overhaul, with transformational potential but high costs. DIB actors describe the initial—and ongoing—difficulties of building capabilities in a place where civil war destroyed almost all of the institutional infrastructure. There are plenty of DIB successes and shortfalls in Liberia to point to, but there have been few attempts to systematically assess DIB projects. Planners and project implementers alike find it difficult to identify which activities led to which outcomes. Coordination between DIB and other security cooperation programs in Liberia is generally efficient because of a variety of informal mechanisms that developed over years of interaction at the embassy level. However, integration and coordination of planning efforts between AFRICOM and the embassy—and incorporation of DIB tools into those plans—remains ad hoc and personality driven, with mixed results.[6]

History of DIB in Liberia

Fourteen years of civil war ravaged Liberia and all but destroyed its entire institutional infrastructure. Its armed forces were a source of predation and destruction; civilian authority and rule of law were nonexistent. In 2003, after a Comprehensive Peace Agreement was signed in Accra, Ghana, the United Nations Security Council authorized the United Nations Mission in Liberia (UNMIL), with a mandate for SSR.[7] UNMIL defined its SSR mandate primarily in terms of police reform, after a Liberian request and UN concurrence that the United States

---

[6]   Material in this section draws on interviews with various members of DIRI, DIILS, DIB representatives, and planners from AFRICOM, OSD, the State Department, and the Michigan National Guard.

[7]   For a comprehensive overview of early security sector transformation efforts, including the Liberian National Police, see Gompert et al., 2007.

should "play a lead role in the restructuring of the army."[8] UNMIL's SSR mandate focused on police reform; the United States agreed to assist with reforming the Armed Forces of Liberia (AFL) and creating a new MoD. At the time, there was little institutional support for the effort within the U.S. interagency.[9] The U.S. ambassador to Liberia, John Blaney, obtained approval from the State Department and special appropriations from Congress. To do the work, the State Department awarded contracts to DynCorp International and Pacific Architects and Engineers. In all, State Department spending on the initial phase of SSR was estimated at around $240 million.[10] Those close to the program suggest that as little as 5 percent of those funds went toward reconstituting the MoD. This early SSR helped produce a 2,000-strong AFL whose mission today is to protect Liberia "against both internal (armed) and external threats, respond to natural (and other) disasters, assist in the reconstruction of [Liberia] and support and participate in regional and international peace."[11]

Near the end of 2009, U.S. SSR efforts in Liberia transitioned to a new phase. AFRICOM took on its first named operation, Operation Onward Liberty (OOL), to do military mentoring with the new AFL. OOL was an AFRICOM-led, State Department–funded military advisory mission with approximately 50 service members who deployed to Liberia in 6–12 month rotations.[12] At the same time, the Michigan National Guard entered into a state partnership with Liberia

---

[8] United Nations Security Council, *Report of the Secretary-General to the Security Council on Liberia*, S/2003/875, September 11, 2003. UNMIL progress reports are available from United Nations Mission in Liberia, "United Nations Documents on UNMIL," web page, undated.

[9] Interview with a former State Department official 20140821-001, August 21, 2014.

[10] Nicolas Cook, *Liberia's Post-War Development: Key Issues and U.S. Assistance*, Washington, D.C.: Congressional Research Service, RL33185, May 19, 2010, pp. 22–23.

[11] Ministry of National Defense (Liberia), *National Defense Strategy of the Republic of Liberia*, February 11, 2014, p. 6.

[12] Marine Corps Forces Africa was the force provider, with most of the troops coming from the Michigan National Guard. See U.S. Africa Command, "Operation Onward Liberty," web page, undated b.

through the SPP.[13] In 2010, DoD DIB programs launched preliminary engagements in Liberia, including the newly formed DIRI and DIILS. The State Department also saw an opportunity to assist, and soon followed with a U.S. defense advisor, a contractor position installed at the MoD.[14]

Based on input from the embassy, DIRI initially focused on working with the MoD to create a national defense strategy.[15] As the relationship developed, so did the DIB team's emphasis on stringent scoping to identify Liberian priorities. DIRI's first work visit was in April–May 2010. From May to October, the team developed and completed the draft National Defense Strategy. It was submitted to the minister in October 2010 but was not given to the president until 2014; President Ellen Johnson Sirleaf approved and signed the National Defense Strategy on February 11, 2014.[16] During this period, DIRI went back every six to eight weeks, focusing on different staff elements as decided by the minister of defense; however, lack of leadership commitment became a problem. When projects neared completion, they failed to go into implementation. In addition to other factors, the president's annual AFL day speeches—in which her policy priorities for the AFL were announced—tended to have a deleterious effect on current work. Rather than finish one task or continue more than one effort at a time, there was a tendency to abandon the previous year's work in pursuit of new priorities emphasized in the speech or from other sources. Reasons cited for the failure to follow through included difficulty getting decisionmakers to focus, reluctance to implement (often out of fear of exposing weakness), and limited training and education levels among

---

[13] SPP is a Title 10–funded, operationally oriented program designed to conduct "little t" training focused on promoting interoperability.

[14] The State Department has multiple defense advisors on the continent. The positions are fluid, with title and specific responsibilities changing based on location. Participants in the program describe it as relationship and opportunity-driven but very influential.

[15] DIRI interview 20140815-001, August 15, 2014.

[16] Liberia Executive Mansion, "At 57th Armed Forces Day Anniversary, Commander-in-Chief Sirleaf Commissions New Liberian Leadership; Urges Them to Lead by Example," press release, February 11, 2014.

MoD personnel. Eventually, DIRI determined there was no value to continuing without a more substantial Liberian investment and took a nine-month break between 2011 and 2012.[17]

In 2012, the opportunity for DIRI to re-engage emerged with a logistics project, one of the four defense management processes that comprise DIRI's core focus.[18] In December 2012, the Liberians outlined a five-year plan for AFL development that identified ten focus areas, three of which fell under logistics. In particular, the MoD identified material maintenance management as a top priority, with a specific focus on vehicles. This aligned with U.S. priorities to help sustain equipment provided to the AFL by the U.S. government, improving the AFL's operational readiness, and complementing OOL's goal of assisting the AFL in training, operations, and logistics.[19] At the time, the AFL had roughly 60 percent more vehicles than it could sustain, and its vehicles hovered at about 18 percent operational readiness. The DIRI regional coordinator and the U.S. defense advisor worked with the country team and devised a strategy to tie maintenance of the existing vehicle fleet to new vehicle allocations through a FMF case. Linking the DIRI project to an FMF vehicle sustainment case for $400,000, along with the threat of pulling out again, persuaded the Liberian government to invest in the project and work began in 2013.[20] This strategy was revised in 2014 when the AFL response to the Ebola outbreak demonstrated the cost associated with maintaining an aging fleet with substandard parts. The 2014 strategy, along with a new FMF case for $3.1 million, called for phased purchases of vehicles, with the AFL demonstrating ability to maintain each batch of vehicles before additional purchases. The strategy required that DIRI assess the AFL plan to ensure its soundness and sustainability before purchasing vehicles.[21]

---

[17] DIRI interview 20141001-001, October 1, 2014.

[18] DIRI, 2013.

[19] DIRI, "Concept for DIRI Support to Liberian Ministry of Defense," June 7, 2012, p. 3.

[20] Email communication with country team official, January 2015.

[21] Email communication with country team official, January 2015.

The other core DIB program in Liberia, DIILS, engaged to help the AFL implement an adapted version of the U.S. Uniform Code of Military Justice (UCMJ).[22] The Liberians had adopted the U.S. UCMJ as-is, but it proved unwieldy for a military whose first lawyers graduated from law school at the end of 2013. U.S. efforts focused on tailoring and modifying those processes to something the Liberians could use. DIILS helped OOL demonstrate to Liberian officials the need for a justice code and disciplinary system with basic legal institutions that aligned with the mission set, composition, and resources of the AFL. From FYs 2011 to 2013, DIILS expended approximately $343,000 on its engagements with Liberia.[23] Together, DIILS and the OOL legal mentors helped launch a more-effective, functional AFL disciplinary system by familiarizing disciplinary board participants with the roles and responsibilities of prosecutors and defense attorneys. Liberians cited these efforts as key to their success completing a disciplinary board that resulted in the conviction and reprimand of two senior officers for bribery and conduct unbecoming an officer.[24]

The U.S. defense advisor's main objective is to help the MoD manage the Liberian military more efficiently and effectively. Currently, the advisor is working on projects related to maintenance, intelligence, the coast guard, and planning. The advisor is an integral member of the ministry staff. Another role the advisor plays is as coach to the Liberians in their interactions with the U.S. military. Together with the Office of Security Cooperation/defense attaché, the advisor has also helped with operational-level projects that require cooperation across the board; for example, the successful deployment of about 35 Liberian soldiers to the United Nations Multidimensional Integrated Stabilization Mission in Mali in 2013.[25]

---

[22] DIILS, 2013, p. 4.

[23] This is operations and maintenance funding. Email communication with DIILS personnel, January 2015.

[24] Email communication with DIILS personnel, January 2015, and DIILS interview 20141113-001, November 13, 2014.

[25] State Department interview 20141023-002, October 23, 2014.

Cooperation Objectives and Strategy for Liberia

A stable security sector is the top priority for Liberia in the AFRICOM FY 2015 CCP. The Liberia CCP identifies an end state for the Liberian defense sector as having the "ability to sustain, maintain, and train its force for operations designated by civilian authority to assure the peace and stability of Liberia."[26] The CCP notes the role that defense coop-eration activities play in supporting broader U.S. government objec-tives and emphasizes the role of DIB. The AFRICOM TCP's LOE to strengthen defense *capabilities* applies to Liberia, and the Liberia CCP includes a country-level objective to strengthen defense *institu-tions*, with associated focus areas and milestones.[27] Various DIB tools, including the core programs DIRI and DIILS, are listed as resources, but without substantial discussion of when or where these might be applied.[28]

In principle, the AFRICOM country desk officer develops the CCP for Liberia in coordination with the embassy's ICS; the two plans inform each other. ICS and CCP development runs in parallel, with embassy and AFRICOM coordination between May and October, producing a final ICS in December and a signed CCP in January.[29] The embassy's Office of Security Cooperation chief and the senior defense official (SDO)/defense attaché (DATT) synchronize the ICS and CCP objectives, with the AFRICOM desk officer as the principal refiner to ensure that AFRICOM priorities are addressed.[30] In addition to the ICS/CCP development, the embassy would typically lead a yearly planning conference for Liberia—the Country Coordination Meet-ing—convened in country or at AFRICOM headquarters in Stuttgart, Germany. However, the Ebola outbreak in 2014 disrupted regular planning processes in the affected countries, including Liberia. AFRI-

---

[26] U.S. Africa Command, undated a.

[27] Please see footnote 40 on page 49 for updated TCP information.

[28] U.S. Africa Command, undated a.

[29] Hooper, 2013.

[30] Email communication with country team official, January 2015.

COM planners suggested these meetings were becoming less frequent and might switch to a case-by-case basis given the demand signal.[31]

In practice, integration of planning efforts remains limited. AFRICOM faces heavy rotation and staff officers who come in without prior experience. Some have limited familiarity with command and embassy planning processes, the content of the plans, or even the countries themselves. Planners find it difficult to align given different time horizons and turnover rates. Another source of friction was that "everything is always in draft" at AFRICOM. OSD staff stated they had often requested to see plans or requirements, but found little forthcoming in the past.[32] For instance, until the end of 2014, AFRICOM did not have a published CCP for Liberia. Part of this delay came from internally shifting requirements; planners described frequently changing guidance on what types of plans and products to develop. As a result, planners ended up with different types of unpublished plans without a way to "compare apples to apples."[33]

DIB tools have yet to be effectively incorporated into AFRICOM planning.[34] DIRI and DIILS both contribute to AFRICOM planning processes—DIRI primarily through the SDO/DATT's input and DIILS through direct consultation with the command's Office of Legal Counsel. However, two main challenges undermined coordination. First, there were conflicting views over how AFRICOM should use the DIB tools. A number of AFRICOM staff described an ideal top-down architecture that would give the command "complete control" over DIB programs, with supervision on the ground provided by embassy representatives.[35] The DIB programs viewed themselves as a

---

[31] Email communication with AFRICOM J5 personnel, January 2015.

[32] OSD also mentioned concerns with the ICSs; while the SDO/DATT is supposed to represent DoD equities in the plans, it often lacks the visibility that OSD has. As a result, OSD does not know if key functional areas of significance to the department have been taken into account. Phone interview with OSD personnel, October 3, 2014.

[33] AFRICOM interview 20141107-001, November 7, 2014.

[34] This will likely change with the new AFRICOM DIB Management Office, created in 2014; this case reflects the planning process through 2014.

[35] AFRICOM interview 20140813-001, August 13, 2014.

tool or resource that AFRICOM could request from OSD based on priority needs. Reflecting this ambiguity over how to best leverage the DIB programs, DIRI was included in the CCP, but simply listed as one of a number of tools without substantive discussion. DIRI personnel described limited interaction with AFRICOM and reported receiving little guidance or interest from the command.[36] Second, lack of a clear view of all existing DIB tools and ongoing activities in Liberia created the risk of duplication. For example, although DIRI and the U.S. defense advisor had worked with the MoD to develop and publish a National Defense Strategy in 2014, the FY 2015–2019 CCP included a milestone for the MoD to develop and submit a National Defense Strategy by the end of FY 2015, with the Office of Security Cooperation chief/AFRICOM J5 as the primary executors for the milestone.[37]

On the other hand, DIRI incorporation into the Liberian ICS stands out as a success story. The State Department's ICS for Liberia describes a stable security sector and respect for rule of law as its first priority for Liberia. Each priority, or goal, has nested objectives and sub-objectives. For FYs 2015 to 2017, the objective of a more professionalized AFL includes improving capacity in providing strategic guidance and functional support to the AFL. Indicators and milestones include specific DIRI projects and associated metrics.[38] This success was attributed to the strong personal relationships between the DIRI regional coordinator, U.S. defense advisor, current ambassador, and SDO/DATT.[39] DIILS, on the other hand, lacked those relationships. Although DIILS was more closely connected with AFRICOM, they were not well represented in the CCP or at all in the ICS. DIILS personnel pointed to the need for inclusion in strategic plans to ensure

---

[36] DIRI interview 20141119-001, November 19, 2014.

[37] U.S. Africa Command, undated a, and email communication with country team, State Department, and DIRI personnel, January 2015.

[38] Email communication with country team official, January 2015.

[39] DIRI interview 20141119-001, November 19, 2014.

ongoing access to countries when personnel turnover occurs at AFRI-COM or the embassies.[40]

Harmonization of Liberian Efforts

All DIB efforts involve a wide array of actors, but the web of DIB actors in Liberia is surprisingly complex given the small size of the AFL and MoD. Harmonization begins at the policy level in the Office of the Secretary of Defense through the Deputy Assistant Secretary of Defense (DASD) for Security Cooperation and DASD for African Affairs, who provide functional and regional oversight for DIB in Africa. The DASD for Security Cooperation recently began holding monthly DIB calls with all of the core DIB programs. Both DIILS and DIRI program managers described this as a valuable coordination tool. The DIB program implementers in Liberia had relatively little direct interaction on the ground and said the calls created visibility and synergy; one program manager described it as the first time they had systematically looked at what other DIB programs were doing.[41]

The embassy country team is the focal point for coordinating activities executed in Liberia. Whenever DIRI teams went into the country, the ambassador was briefed in advance. Typically, the DIRI teams held an in-brief and out-brief with the ambassador, deputy chief of mission, or SDO/DATT. The State defense advisor was also an integral part of facilitating DIRI's trips and viewed one of his goals as helping move DIRI forward. As the former Office of Security Cooperation chief/SDO in Liberia himself, he understood the range of DIB resources available and made recommendations to the country team based on his knowledge.[42] The positive relationship partially resulted from the advisor's close personal friendship with the DIRI regional

---

[40] DIILS interview 20141113-001, November 13, 2014.

[41] DIILS interview 20141113-001, November 13, 2014.

[42] Both State and DoD personnel in interviews described MoDA as a more robust form of DIRI, where advisors go on short rotations to special functional areas within ministries, whereas State defense advisors form long-term, catch-all relationships and were coordinated across the MoD.

coordinator. The advisor and the DIRI team shared ideas and offered suggestions for projects based on gaps they identified.[43]

Individual personalities have affected the quality of coordination in Liberia. For example, early differences of opinion existed between AFRICOM planners, DIB managers, and the SDO/DATT about the balance to draw between U.S. and partner-nation priorities—for example, whether AFRICOM or the embassy was best positioned to provide overarching policy guidance appropriate for the country.[44] Communication subsequently improved; however, this situation highlights the impediment that poor relationships and a lack of harmonization can present.

On the other hand, an example of effective coordination is the close working relationship that emerged between DIRI and OOL. The OOL mentors and their counterparts became integral members of DIRI's working group. During engagements, the DIRI country lead would sit down once a week with the OOL officer in charge and coordinate. They would share agendas and participant lists ahead of visits to deconflict. DIRI members described the military mentors as eager to help and key facilitators of follow up between trips.[45]

The other core DIB program in Liberia, DIILS, coordinated differently. DIILS activities were coordinated with the legal advisor to OOL rather than through the embassy (reportedly at the Office of Security Cooperation chief's instruction).[46] While country clearance and administrative items ran through the Office of Security Cooperation, DIILS orchestrated its mobile programs through the OOL coordinator rather than the embassy or Liberians directly. In its own view, DIILS functioned as a "service provider," receiving information indirectly from the embassy through the OOL mentor who participated in embassy meetings and raised issues on DIILS's behalf if necessary. Part of this arrangement sprang from having a Michigan National Guard

---

[43] DIRI interview 20141031-001, October 31, 2014.

[44] DIRI interview 20141119-001, November 19, 2014; and former country team official interview 20141023-001, October 23, 2014.

[45] DIRI interview 20141001-001, October 1, 2014.

[46] DIILS interview 20141113-001, November 13, 2014.

lawyer serve as the bilateral affairs officer in the embassy; this helped cement the DIILS relationship with SPP and OOL.

DIRI and DIILS also established a cooperative working arrangement, developed in part through their coordination in Liberia. DIRI serves as an entrance into new countries, helping to convince the partner nation of the need for DIILS engagement at lower levels. In Liberia and elsewhere, DIILS sees its primary focus as falling below the institutional level; DIRI sees its role as identifying ways to support those gains at lower levels and find ways to institutionalize at higher levels.[47] These observations underscore the fact that, in a small country like Liberia, institutional, operational, and tactical levels blend. At times this makes for effective partnerships, as it did in Liberia, where DIILS worked effectively with AFRICOM, OOL, and other DIB programs by straddling the seam between institutional and operational activities. At other times, it may lead to confusion. As one respondent said, "The whole notion of DIB is U.S.-centric, it's the idea that you can draw an artificial line and call the part above 'DIB' and the part below '[Security Force Assistance].'"[48] A definition of institutions that keeps the focus on the rules and norms required for good governance, rather than a focus on the organizations that form around those rules, can help avoid artificially imposed categories.

By 2014, the panoply of DIB actors in Liberia included other countries. A UK advisor complemented the OOL mentoring team and, in 2014, the Liberian president credited three major non-African partners in rebuilding the AFL: the United States, the United Kingdom, and China.[49] China is considered a "major training nation" in Liberia; in 2014, Liberia reportedly had nine officers in the United States for training, 16 in China, and a handful in Nigeria and elsewhere.[50] In

---

[47] DIRI interview 20141119-001, November 19, 2014; and DIILS interview 20141113-001, November 13, 2014.

[48] DIILS interview 20141113-001, November 13, 2014.

[49] Liberia Executive Mansion, "Speech by H.E. Madam Ellen Johnson Sirleaf, President and Commander-in-Chief of the Armed Forces of Liberia on the 57th Armed Forces Day," Speeches, February 11, 2014.

[50] Communication with DIRI personnel, August 2014.

general, though, Chinese engagement is limited to equipment dona-
tion and training in Chinese schools. The U.S. defense advisor and
DIRI were the only actors consistently engaged with the MoD.[51]

Partner Nation Prioritization

In 2010, Liberia was a top priority for OSD and AFRICOM—a
rare consensus in a region where they frequently disagreed on which
countries to prioritize until the SGI selected six countries for targeted
capacity-building efforts.[52] Recognizing the need for engagement at
the institutional level in concert with the operationally oriented OOL
mission, Liberia was one of the first country engagements for a brand-
new DIRI. The program sent out nominations to the combatant commands, Joint Staff, and OSD, asking them for their priority countries.
All three entities listed Liberia, leading to DIRI's initial engagement in
2010. DIILS began its engagement in Liberia in 2010 as well.

Since 2010, Liberia was re-evaluated and continues to be a priority. While Liberia is not mentioned as a DIB focus country in the
Guidance for Employment of the Force, the FY 2015 CCP notes that
Liberia continues to receive the largest amount of DIB resources in
Sub-Saharan Africa.[53] The initial OOL mission had a five-year mandate. In 2014, the DASD for African Affairs agreed to renew OOL for
the next one to two years, albeit on a reduced scale, indicating its continued importance.[54] DIRI also remained engaged, although the Ebola
crisis halted momentum on the ground in 2014. DIB team visits have
not occurred since early 2014; while there was some discussion of reengaging via teleconference, efforts remained on ice throughout most
of the year while attention focused on containing the immediate crisis.

---

[51] State Department interview 20141023-002, October 23, 2014.

[52] OSD interview 20141003-001, October 3, 2014; and AFRICOM interview 20140818-
001, August 18, 2014. Also see The White House, 2014.

[53] U.S. Africa Command, undated a.

[54] OOL will continue in 2015 in a pared-down form (15 mentors) and shift from Marine
Corps Forces Africa to U.S. Army Africa as force provider, with all forces drawn from the
Michigan National Guard. Michigan National Guard interview 20141016-001, October 16,
2014.

In 2014, DIILS phased out its engagement based on organizational decisions to reprioritize elsewhere and concerns over Liberian absorptive capacity for additional engagement at the time.

There is concern about the future of DIB efforts in Liberia, particularly with the long break in 2014. Four years of expending time and resources with limited progress, frequent setbacks, and inconclusive projects led some to conclude efforts were just "limping along." At some point, the burden needs to shift to Liberians to prove they can and will handle it.

Others took the long view. Liberia emerged from a devastating civil war. Building institutions and capacity from scratch takes time and patience. For a decade, the AFL lacked its own leadership; until early 2014, a Nigerian general served as officer in charge of the AFL. In February 2014, the AFL's first flag officer, Brigadier General Daniel Ziankahn assumed command as Chief of Staff. Liberians have replaced ECOWAS officers at the brigade level as well. Liberian leadership is a necessary step toward ownership of the capabilities that U.S. counterparts have worked to help create.

Assessment

Virtually all of the actors conducting DIB in Liberia identified assessments as their greatest challenge. Efforts to assess DIB activities have remained ad hoc and largely anecdotal. Success stories abound, but so do shortfalls and challenges. DIB practitioners described their difficulties measuring these shortfalls and challenges, which in turn obscured the key factors contributing to success or failure. U.S. observers who have spent significant time working with the Liberian government uniformly describe the AFL and MoD as Liberia's strongest institutions today. Intuitively, this attests to the time, resources, and effort expended on DIB in Liberia, yet it remains difficult to assess the influence of specific projects.[55]

---

[55] It should be noted that MoDs and militaries may not have the same degree of interaction with the civilian world that police departments, tax bureaus, and other such governmental services have. Therefore, these other services may be the object of political battles and could be more likely to encounter issues of corruption or graft; MoDs and militaries are not immune from these problems, but could have some degree of insulation.

At the theater level, there was no standard assessment process for Liberia at the time of this writing, nor has there been any detailed assessment of Liberia. Several factors contributed to the delay. One challenge was ongoing limitations to AFRICOM's ability to assess institutional effects. There were few, if any, efforts at systematic assessment of activities associated with DIB (or with the command's sixth LOE, to strengthen defense capabilities) until the command created a new DIB manager in the summer of 2014. Planners expressed concern that reliance on anecdotal evidence in lieu of rigorous assessments was insufficient justification for continuing to expend resources and conduct projects.[56]

In general, assessment of the effectiveness of activities depended on team feedback. Two primary feedback mechanisms were communication between the country director and the SDO/DATT and after-action reporting from teams on the ground. However, the efficacy of these mechanisms varied with the strength of individual relationships and the quality of trip reports. Among the DIB programs, trip reports were the primary feedback mechanism. At the end of each trip, DIRI sent a report to the embassy, AFRICOM, and OSD. At the end of each report, the regional coordinator articulated what was needed next and provided cost estimates, which led to discussions with DIRI and OSD leadership. Both DIRI and OSD described these trip reports as valuable opportunities to receive guidance (DIRI) and provide feedback (OSD).[57] However, none of the DIB actors on the ground reported receiving specific or regular guidance from higher levels, with the exception of DIILS, which coordinated closely with AFRICOM.

At the country level, DIB practitioners expressed similar challenges. First, with the number of actors and projects at each stage of the capacity-building process, it can be difficult to figure out which pieces lead to which parts of the outcome. For example, a basic metric for DIRI's vehicle maintenance project was whether Liberian vehicle readiness improved. It did, but was it the result of DIRI's efforts, the

---

[56] AFRICOM interview 20141107-001, November 7, 2014.

[57] DIRI interview 20141119-001, November 19, 2014; and OSD interview 20141003-001, October 3, 2014.

FMF case that bought parts and provided training, or Liberian motivation? DIILS practitioners expressed a similar concern. While these distinctions do not matter for gauging Liberian progress, they may matter when programs are called on to demonstrate their value added within the U.S. DIB enterprise. Another countrywide challenge was follow up. Long breaks between visits tended to lead to inaction. An SPP tactical contact team described reengaging every six months to retrain on the same thing, only to go back each time and discover nothing had been done.[58] Moreover, Liberians were often not employed in the capacity for which they had been trained. A member of the country team described using IMET to train AFL electricians, only to find that they were not being used as electricians two years later.[59]

Attempts to build milestones or metrics into DIB program project plans remained elusive. Respondents reported having limited information on which metrics were desired or how to construct them. DIRI project plans developed in conjunction with, and signed by, their Liberian counterparts included process, output, and outcome metrics; however, these were not tracked. Unwillingness to reveal failures may have translated into a reluctance to report metrics on both sides. Yet, in the case of Liberia, dedicated DIB efforts under extremely limiting circumstances did lead to numerous instances of successful capacity building—for instance, DIILS' success in assisting the AFL to set up a functioning disciplinary board.

Liberia: Insights and Lessons for DIB

A decade of SSR in Liberia, including five years of concentrated DIB efforts, reveals best practices to replicate and challenges to mitigate. Best practices include the following:

- Coordination mechanisms on the ground between and across institutional and operational projects. Informal mechanisms, such as including OOL mentors and their AFL counterparts in the DIRI working group, helped to ensure that capacity-building

---

[58] Michigan National Guard interview 20141016-001, October 16, 2014.

[59] Michigan National Guard interview 20141016-001, October 16, 2014.

efforts at different levels remained in sync. Similarly, close coordination between DIRI and the defense advisor maintained complementarity of DoD and State Department efforts.

- As noted elsewhere, time and relationships are critical to DIB. The presence of a long-term U.S. defense advisor embedded at the MoD, along with OOL mentors on the ground for six to 12 months, built trust, deepened understanding of Liberian interests and institutional needs, and helped with monitoring DIB project progress.
- Linking of issues to create leverage and motivate partner nation commitment. Linking DIRI's vehicle maintenance project to an FMF case for new vehicles and spare parts incentivized AFL progression toward sustainable fleet management.

Despite these bright spots, several persistent challenges undermined progress:

- Inconsistent partner nation involvement and lack of leadership commitment. Inconsistent commitment from MoD and AFL leadership and changing political priorities often resulted in delayed or failed project implementation. Time may be the best remedy for this challenge; ECOWAS officers from neighboring countries ran the AFL until 2014. As more Liberian leaders come up through the ranks, commitment may become less of an issue. Moreover, issue linkage is an effective way to foster partner nation buy-in—understanding and appropriately leveraging partner incentive structures to maximize partner ownership of initiatives. Our recommendations in Chapter Five should provide ways to help DoD and the State Department identify these incentives and link them to DIB objectives.
- Weak partner nation absorptive capacity. Small size and low capacity within the AFL and MoD civilian staff meant that even simple projects were often more than the Liberians could implement or sustain. This was particularly acute within the MoD, where assistant ministers often lacked basic education, training,

or authority to operate.[60] This means that even in post-conflict DIB programs where sweeping reform is possible, efforts must still be incremental and project goals should not be too ambitious. Long-term relationship building and knowledge of national and local political, institutional, and social factors are important. Incorporating more-structured approaches for assessing country-level indicators, like those discussed in Chapter Three, can help identify which engagements will be most viable.

- Insufficient visibility across the spectrum of security cooperation/ DIB tools. Limited awareness of various DIB activities can lead to missed opportunities or duplicative efforts. Our recommendations in Chapter Five should help improve AFRICOM and U.S. embassy awareness of which DIB tools are available and which DIB projects are already underway or completed in the partner country.

- Assessments continue to be ad hoc and largely anecdotal—successes and failures are not adequately captured and there are no clear metrics against which to measure progress. This is an area where best practices from other DIB practitioners might be leveraged as a model; for example, the French practice of signing a convention with the partner nation stating project duration, goals, intermediate objectives, and associated activities and timelines.[61] Currently, project reporting and trip reports provide feedback, but there is no standard format or central repository for reporting. Adopting a universal tracking system like the Global Theater Security Cooperation Management Information System could address this challenge.

---

[60] DIRI interview 20141001-001, October 1, 2014.

[61] See Chapter Four.

Libya Case Study

Plans for DIB in Libya were in motion for several years, but actual institution building had not yet occurred as of 2014.[62] Despite a promising period in the immediate aftermath of the Libyan revolution and Colonel Muammar Gaddafi's fall from power, conditions deteriorated rapidly after the traumatic events of September 2012 in Benghazi, when a militant attack killed the U.S. ambassador, Christopher Stevens, along with three other Americans.

Any future DIB efforts in Libya will likely call for sweeping reform, requiring a substantial commitment of time and resources to rebuild institutions from the ground up. Unlike Liberia, where early SSR efforts at least created a unified institutional framework within which to build capabilities, Libya in 2015 had few, if any, institutional foundations. The absence of viable institutions, partners, or a permissive environment undermines prospects for DIB in Libya. Initial planning focused on SSR and a holistic approach to institution building; DoD DIB practitioners saw an opportunity for a multinational, multi-agency, "clean slate" effort. Yet there is little chance for progress until a minimum level of stability, security, and a basic foundation of governance are established.

Deterioration of security in 2012 severely restricted movement and made it difficult for would-be DIB implementers to engage with their Libyan counterparts. For nearly two years, DIB practitioners described setting aside resources for Libya and preparing to go on a moment's notice, only to be told to hold back.[63] In July 2014, the United States withdrew all its embassy personnel from Tripoli as clashes between rival militias escalated. The country team set up a satellite office in Malta, but the distance further complicated the challenge of coordinating with the international community and identifying viable Libyan partners with whom to engage. Part of the problem was the collapse of government control over institutions post-Gaddafi. Different actors in

---

[62] This section is based on interviews with various members of DIRI, DIILS, AFRICOM, OSD, and UNSMIL.

[63] DIRI interview 20140807-001, August 7, 2014.

the revolution seized different institutions; in August 2014, the interim Libyan government admitted that "the majority of the ministries, institutions, and associations," in Tripoli were not under its control.[64]

History of DIB in Libya

From 1969 to 2011, under Gaddafi's rule, U.S.-Libyan relations were tense, exacerbated by Libya's pursuit of weapons of mass destruction and sponsorship of terrorism. As Libya began to change its behavior in the early 2000s, relations thawed; the United States rescinded Libya's designation as a state sponsor of terrorism in 2006, leading to the lifting of sanctions and restoration of diplomatic relations.[65] However, engagement remained limited until the fall of Gaddafi's regime in 2011. After the NATO-led operation that helped topple Gaddafi, the international community rapidly engaged with the interim Libyan governing structures, which went through three transitional phases by June 2014, when the election of a new Libyan House of Representatives failed to halt the descent into instability and violence among warring factions.[66] In 2011, the United Nations Security Council authorized the United Nations Support Mission for Libya (UNSMIL), with a mandate to assist Libya with a democratic transition, rule of law, SSR, and international assistance coordination. UNSMIL's SSR mandate included efforts to build Libya's national security structure and a defense advisory section that worked with the MoD and the Office of the Chief of the General Staff on a range of capacity-building measures for the Libyan army.[67] By the close of 2014, UN Secretary General Ban Ki-moon noted, "Against a background of continuing violence, the

---

[64] Christopher M. Blanchard, *Libya: Transition and U.S. Policy*, Washington, D.C.: Congressional Research Service, RL33142, September 8, 2014.

[65] Condoleezza Rice, "U.S. Diplomatic Relations with Libya," statement by the U.S. Secretary of State, May 15, 2006.

[66] United Nations Security Council, *Report of the Secretary-General on the United Nations Support Mission in Libya*, S/2014/653, September 5, 2014.

[67] UNSMIL, "Security Sector," web page, undated.

uncertain political situation and lack of effective governance continue to hamper progress in security sector reform."[68]

One of UNSMIL's earliest efforts was to assist the Libyans with drafting a defense white paper, entitled *Towards a Defence White Paper*, which laid out defense priorities and the elements of a future national defense strategy.[69] It was intended to begin the process of defense reform and development, making recommendations for "developing defence policies; implementing defence sector reform; delivering operational capability; and strengthening international defence relations."[70] UNSMIL produced the document in partnership with a Libyan team from the MoD and Office of the Chief of the General Staff; the Libyans insisted that no other nationalities be part of the core team, although other partners were invited to consult throughout the process.[71] UNSMIL invited DoD to participate, so OSD sent a two-person DIRI program team in April 2012. This trip was the first DIRI engagement in Libya; in addition to consulting on the defense paper, the DIRI team used this as an opportunity to conduct an initial assessment and look for potential areas for DIB projects.[72] Following that initial trip, OSD conducted another trip with DIRI in May 2012 with the intent to prepare for a comprehensive assessment and development of a holistic DIB strategy for Libya. In May 2012, OSD and DIRI team members conducted the first scoping trip, where they briefed Ambassador Christopher Stevens and spent five days doing an initial assessment of the situation on the ground.[73] The DIRI team returned to Libya in June 2012 and was planning a fourth trip when the Benghazi attack occurred. June 2012 marked the last presence of any core DIB programs on the ground; however, work on a DIB strategy for Libya continued remotely.

---

[68] United Nations Security Council, 2014, p. 16.

[69] UNSMIL, *Towards a Defence White Paper*, April 2, 2013.

[70] UNSMIL, 2013, p. 1.

[71] Email correspondence with former UNSMIL official, January 2015.

[72] DIRI interview 20140807-001, August 7, 2014.

[73] OSD interview 20141003-001, October 3, 2014.

Although OSD had responsibility for development of the strategy, its intent was to leverage DIRI to conduct the comprehensive assessment. DIRI had established relationships with other actors in Libya through the work on the UNSMIL defense paper and was considered the best suited of the core DIB programs to conduct a holistic evaluation of Libya's defense institutions.[74] Despite repeated talk of resuming engagement, no trips came to fruition. The plug was often pulled at the last minute because of security constraints; on occasion, DIRI teams were within hours of getting on a plane before being told not to travel. As discussed later, other DIB-related activities were planned and sometimes initiated, only to stall.

DIB Objectives and Implementation Planning

The Libya CCP, which was in draft through 2014, identifies an end state for Libya that includes the "institutional foundation for professional armed forces that are loyal to the national government, respect human rights and the laws of armed conflict, protective of the civilian population, maintain territorial integrity, and effectively combat terrorism."[75] The Libya CCP includes a country-level objective to strengthen defense institutions, with focus areas and milestones that address force management, operational capacity, and military justice, among others. Various tools, including DIRI and MoDA, are listed as resources, but without any detailed discussion.[76] Moreover, the only program that was funded against the DIB LOE as of 2014 was IMET.[77] AFRICOM had the funding and the billets—and at least one Libyan officer went to the United States for training in the past year—but with the embassy in Malta, there was no way to screen additional candidates or to find a partner on the Libyan side to identify candidates.

In 2013, AFRICOM began planning for an operation similar to OOL in Liberia. The intent was for "a multinational effort to support

---

[74] Communication with OSD and DIRI personnel, January 2015.

[75] Libya CCP.

[76] Libya CCP.

[77] AFRICOM interview 20141107-001, November 7, 2014.

modest defense institution building and the development of security forces,"[78] with the UK, Italy, and Turkey joining the United States as partners. The AFRICOM plan had two LOEs: one to establish and train the Libyan General Purpose Force and one to conduct DIB.

For its part of the General Purpose Force training effort, AFRI-COM planned to oversee the training of 6,000–8,000 Libyans in Bulgaria, but the effort quickly foundered. First, Libyan funding was not forthcoming, which was a key proviso of the arrangement. In early 2014, a U.S. congressional notification indicated that the Libyan government had committed to pay $600 million for the General Purpose Force training program.[79] Congress approved the foreign military sales request for the program; however, the Libyans were unable or unwilling to fund the letter of request they signed with the U.S. government. Second, the UK, Italy, and Turkey had already conducted their own training without much success. Problems included inability to pay the trainees and nowhere for them to go once the training was done. They had no access to weapons—the militias controlled the armories—and there was no functioning MoD to oversee their sustainment. Moreover, the Libyans themselves disagreed over key points, such as inclusion of revolutionary fighters or the legitimacy of the General Purpose Force, questioning whether then–Prime Minister Ali Zeidan should have requested multilateral assistance to build the security forces.[80] As initial efforts to train the General Purpose Force stalled, AFRICOM Commander Gen. David M. Rodriguez advised OSD to focus security cooperation efforts and funds on other willing partners.[81]

The second LOE, to build defense institutions, came from AFR-ICOM's recognition that institutionalized support was necessary to sustain any operational-level gains. Initially, AFRICOM developed institutional requirements without engaging OSD or the core DIB

---

[78] David M. Rodriguez, "2014 AFRICOM Posture Statement," Statement Before the Senate Armed Services Committee, March 6, 2014, p. 10.

[79] Blanchard, 2014, p. 11.

[80] Frederic Wehrey, *Ending Libya's Civil War: Reconciling Politics, Rebuilding Security*, Carnegie Endowment for International Peace, September 2014, pp. 25–26.

[81] AFRICOM interview 20140818-001, August 18, 2014.

programs. The first attempt was an expansive rebuilding effort with a scale and scope too ambitious for Libyan absorptive capacity. Eventually, OSD pitched a scaled-back concept that the command adopted. While OSD played a critical role in developing the final LOE, initial disagreement over what it should entail, who should implement it, and the chain of command in country (i.e., who the DIB programs would report to) were sources of friction. Despite these issues of authority, scope, and complexity, AFRICOM and OSD shared a common goal and reached consensus.[82] Ultimately, they agreed that DIRI would shape and implement the DIB LOE.[83]

For its part, DIRI planned to do something new. Libya presented an opportunity to do a comprehensive assessment and create a holistic DIB strategy designed to integrate all of the appropriate DIB programs and resources. OSD asked DIRI to assess the current baseline of MoD and Libyan Armed Forces institutional capacity; identify UNSMIL, NATO, and other partner DIB efforts; and then highlight gaps remaining between these efforts and Libyan requirements. These gaps would form the focal point for recommended U.S. DIB efforts. The Libya assessment concept also formalized reporting requirements, calling for interim reports on findings as well as a final written report of findings and recommendations for a way forward.[84]

The concept called for an assessment of the MoD and the Libyan Armed Forces capacity in key functional areas, including logistics, resource management, military justice, and human resource management. Recommended DIB efforts would target the needed capacity to sustain and manage the Libyan Armed Forces with emphasis on the soldiers trained through the General Purpose Force effort.[85] The concept called for coordination with partner DIB actors (such as the UN and NATO), consideration of other DoD DIB tools, and integration with other capacity-building capabilities such as Section 1206

---

[82] Country team interview 20150317-001, March 17, 2015.

[83] Communication with OSD personnel, January 2015.

[84] DIRI, *Concept for Defense Institution Building (DIB) Assessment in Libya*, undated.

[85] DIRI, undated.

and Section 1207 funds.[86] Moreover, the long-term DIB strategy that would come after the assessment explicitly called for identification of objectives aligned to LOEs, associated timelines, tasks, milestones, and standards defining satisfactory task completion.[87] By the end of 2014, the assessment had not been conducted because of a lack of a permissive environment or viable Libyan partners.

Other DIB programs planned to engage in parallel to the DIRI effort. For several years, DIILS set funding aside for a scoping visit to Libya. DIILS was slated to go on a familiarization trip with AFRICOM in the summer of 2012, but as the security situation deteriorated, access was denied.[88] While the DoD regional centers have not conducted any bilateral events, the Libyans did participate in multilateral events in the first days after the revolution, sending representatives to the regional centers' Senior Leader Seminar, NextGen, and other forums. That early engagement was also subsequently suspended.[89] Finally, Illinois was proposed as a state partner for Libya through the SPP, but that too was shelved as security and stability in Libya deteriorated.[90]

Harmonization

Like all partner nations, there is a complex array of actors involved with DIB in Libya. In some ways, the fragile political security environment in Libya forced closer harmonization among these actors than in other countries. In other ways, the chaotic post-conflict environment made coordination challenging, particularly among the United States, NATO, and UN elements that operated in Libya with different mandates and objectives. Within DoD, harmonization begins at the policy level, with OSD providing functional and regional oversight for DIB in Africa. Over the past three years, OSD coordinated closely with the National Security Council (NSC), the State Department, NATO, and

---

[86] DIRI, undated.

[87] DIRI, undated.

[88] DIILS interview 20141113-001, November 13, 2014.

[89] ACSS interview 20140819-001, August 19, 2014.

[90] Email communication with AFRICOM personnel, January 2015.

other partners. During the early days of engagement in 2012, DIRI helped gather information for U.S. entities that were "thirsting for information" from the ground in Libya. The DIRI team engaged with OSD, State, the U.S. Agency for International Development, and other governmental agencies, providing information after each trip and conducting roundtable Q&A sessions.[91]

At the theater level in a steady state, the AFRICOM country desk officer develops the CCP for Libya in parallel with the embassy's ICS (as is done in Liberia). The intent is to synchronize the two plans; however, because of the chaos in Libya, both plans remained in draft throughout 2014.[92] When the country team relocated to Malta, staff numbers dropped sharply, leaving fewer than half a dozen personnel engaged with diplomatic activities. With such limited capacity, the team was not adequately staffed to produce an ICS.[93] As elsewhere, the main focal point for harmonizing and coordinating DIB activities in country is the country team. Respondents cited constraints on the country team as one of the primary impediments to conducting DIB in Libya. With a small team and an insecure environment, ability to accommodate DIB actors (including helping them to move around the country securely) was extremely difficult.[94] The decision to keep force protection responsibilities under Chief of Mission authority—rather than under combatant command authorities—was a limiting factor; supporting DIB teams for even a week or two on the ground was beyond the team's capacity.[95] Moreover, the team's relocation to Malta predictably complicated efforts to access the country or identify Libyan partners with whom to engage.

In Libya's case, non-U.S. actors had significant DIB responsibilities. Although UNSMIL had the lead for SSR in Libya, it was reportedly understaffed for the task. Some suggest that since UNSMIL had

---

[91] DIRI interview 20140807-001, August 7, 2014.

[92] AFRICOM interview 20141107-001, November 7, 2014.

[93] Country team interview 20150317-001, March 17, 2015.

[94] DIRI interview 20140807-001, August 7, 2014.

[95] Country team interview 20150317-001, March 17, 2015.

the lead for SSR, the U.S. government played a more passive role planning for DIB in Libya. The European Union was also an active partner in post-conflict reconstruction, helping Libyan authorities secure land, sea, and air borders with an integrated border assistance mission that disbanded in early 2015.[96] NATO also attempted to play a DIB role; however, it ran into numerous challenges. NATO was asked to assist the Libyans with building an NSC-type structure, but despite effective NATO-DoD coordination, NATO never quite managed to make it on the ground in Libya.[97] Bilateral DIB efforts included British advisors embedded in the Libyan MoD, but the Libyans did not meaningfully engage with them and expressed little interest in their advice.[98]

In general, little DIB coordination occurred between OSD and the UN, and AFRICOM planners reported "minimal" interaction with international or multinational organizations in Libya.[99] Most of the UN-U.S. coordination occurred through the country team— UNSMIL reported working closely with the embassy. Members from the country team participated in UNSMIL working groups that convened regularly around each of the Security Sector Advisory and Coordination Division's focus areas.[100] Another bright spot was the early and effective integration between DIRI program managers and the UN, with the invitation to participate in the UNSMIL defense white paper development. This helped strengthen relationships with the key players in the international community, the embassy team, and the Libyan government. Unfortunately, the defense white paper failed to

---

[96] European Union External Action, 2015.

[97] Country team interview 20150317-001, March 17, 2015; and OSD interview 20150113-001, January 13, 2015.

[98] Country team interview 20150317-001, March 17, 2015.

[99] OSD interview 20150113-001, January 13, 2015; and AFRICOM interview 20141107-001, November 7, 2014.

[100] Email communication with former UNSMIL official, January 2015. The focus areas included national security architecture; arms and ammunition management; police; defense; border security; and disarmament, demobilization, and reintegration. See UNSMIL, undated.

achieve its desired effect among the Libyan authorities; instead, it was largely disregarded.[101]

The comprehensive DIB assessment conducted by OSD and DIRI program managers in 2013 highlighted an ongoing coordination issue between policy and theater levels: the need for improved communication between OSD, which better understands State and DoD DIB-related capabilities and programs, and AFRICOM, which better understands partner country requirements. In the case of Libya planning, military officers without DIB training were attempting to outline requirements for DIB programs without fully understanding their options. As one respondent observed, "we're asked to come up with ways to support DIB but we are just lining up facts and arguments for the Commander to support pursuit of national assets. . . . The groups that do this work are above the [AFRICOM] level."[102] Lack of personal relationships may have contributed to this problem in the Libya case; whereas some DIB practitioners cited close working relationships with AFRICOM as key to success in Liberia, AFRICOM's relationship with DIRI program managers vis-à-vis Libya was reportedly limited. This highlights the need for a system that enables effective planning to continue irrespective of individual interactions.

Partner Nation Selection and Prioritization

Libya came up as a nomination for DIB prioritization soon after the revolution in 2011. It was a post-conflict environment with a clear need for institution building, and it was a major U.S. priority. The NSC solicited feedback on appropriate next steps in Libya, and OSD proposed a DIB effort spearheaded by DIRI and MoDA, which the NSC accepted.[103] Because Libya was such a high priority in the aftermath of the revolution, the nomination happened as a "collective conversation" among the different interagency partners.

By all accounts, things changed substantially in the wake of the 2012 attack on the U.S. diplomatic compound in Benghazi. The attack

---

[101] Country team interview 20150317-001, March 17, 2015.

[102] AFRICOM interview 20141107-001, November 7, 2014.

[103] OSD interview 20150113-001, January 13, 2015.

was a significant, emotional event for the United States that had immediate consequences for engagement. Access was severely restricted and, as time passed, the trail went "from hot to lukewarm." In the eyes of some, the restrictions were self-imposed—other partners remained more engaged on the ground. Over time the focus shifted to re-establishing diplomatic relations, with DIB efforts remaining in limbo. Since then, plans have remained suspended, but AFRICOM and OSD planners have kept an eye on Libya. AFRICOM has kept a country desk officer for Libya, despite the lack of current engagement. OSD and DIRI describe maintaining a state of "warm ready" for the past two years, coordinating with the State Department, NATO, nongovernmental organizations, and other groups.[104]

Initially, Libya appeared to be the perfect scenario for DIB prioritization—there was a clear U.S. objective and perceived needs of the partner country. DIB managers stress the need for a confluence of interest between the U.S. and the partner, and this certainly appeared present in the early days of post-Gaddafi Libya. Throughout 2014 and into 2015, there was still a substantial amount of policy interest and focus on planning for Libya. Yet, given the uncertainty over what would come next, DIB planning remains on hold.

Libya: Insights and Lessons for DIB

Given the inability as of yet to implement DIB projects in Libya, it is difficult to point to best practices. Yet several examples emerge from the planning efforts that did take place.

First was DIRI's potential role as an overarching/coordinating program for DIB assessments. Plans for a comprehensive DIB strategy point to the need for a designated program or team to conduct initial assessments. It remains unclear whether this should be a core DIRI role. DIRI has the expertise, but is structured and resourced as a regular DIB program.

Second, a comprehensive DIB strategy creates visibility and helps prevent duplicative efforts. Planning metrics and standards for suc-

---

[104]OSD interview 20141003-001, October 3, 2014; and DIRI interview 20140807-001, August 7, 2014.

cessful task completion in advance, including timelines, is a major step toward establishing objective monitoring processes and improving assessments. In Chapter Five, we recommend that OSD organize a pilot effort in a single African country as a model for future DIB efforts, building on this best practice from the Libya case. This pilot effort includes a five-year DIB plan, built on a comprehensive baseline assessment, with inputs from across the U.S. government, partner nation, and international partners.

Third, coordinating across multiple actors in complex environments is challenging, but can be done effectively. Libya's chaotic and volatile environment heightened the need for close coordination. In post-conflict areas where the UN has a mandate for SSR, it is important that DoD maintain visibility of effort. This is a relative bright spot for Libya, with close country team integration into UNSMIL planning efforts and DoD participation in the UNSMIL defense white paper. Yet, there is room for improvement. Communication can improve between OSD and AFRICOM—the former bringing insights on DIB-related capabilities and the latter bringing insights on country-level requirements. Additionally, relocating the U.S. team to Malta while most of the other missions moved to Tunis meant that coordination with international partners had to be conducted remotely.

Conducting DIB in a post-conflict environment that is still transitioning is particularly risky and challenging. What role can (or should) DIB have in less-permissive environments? On the one hand, the partner nation's ability and willingness to engage should factor into decisions about the U.S. level of involvement. On the other hand, an overly risk-averse approach may limit the ability to effectively engage. Both OSD and the core DIB programs viewed the lack of personnel on the ground when the environment was more permissive as a lost opportunity.[105] Moreover, a lack of viable Libyan partners created a potentially insurmountable challenge in the near term. Planning for DIB assumed that the Libyan government would allow the U.S. presence in Libya, fund security sector assistance activities, and accept and cooperate with

---

[105] Interview with OSD personnel, October 3, 2014, and interview with DIRI personnel, August 7, 2014

proposed activities.[106] These assumptions did not hold and the more fundamental criterion of a unified Libyan government has yet to be achieved. Where partners have engaged—with the defense white paper and British advisors in the MoD—they have met with resistance or indifference. Basic issues of Libyan capacity and willingness to build institutions must be resolved to implement DIB.

---

[106]Libya CCP.

CHAPTER FIVE

Findings and Recommendations

As discussed in Chapter One, our goal for this project was to assess DIB efforts in Africa and provide insights on possible improvements to planning and execution. In this chapter, we gather insights from the three components of our research: our review of DIB-related best practices and official guidance for Africa, our overview of DIB programs in Africa, and our case studies.

Findings and Recommendations from Our Review of DIB-Related Best Practices and Official Guidance for Africa

Although the use of the term DIB is relatively recent, it is closely related to other concepts that have been employed for several decades, such as SSR, defense sector reform, and SSG. Many of the best practices developed around these various concepts are relevant to DIB. Understanding, for example, how to tailor programs to specific conditions of partner nations, gaining buy-in from partner leadership, incorporating civil society considerations, and establishing monitoring and evaluation techniques should greatly improve DIB effectiveness. We found little evidence, however, that these lessons were being systematically documented to support DIB planners and implementers.

We also found that although some formal guidance exists and communication goes on, the guidance is insufficient and communication is overly ad hoc, given the complexity of DIB and how it relates to security cooperation more generally.

Our research also indicated that DIB is a stepping stone to other U.S. defense objectives in Africa. In analyzing more than a dozen U.S. government strategic guidance documents for Africa, we found that two of the six main defense-related objectives are, in effect, DIB. Moreover, these two DIB objectives have an impact on other defense-related U.S. strategic objectives, as they improve the partner nation's defense forces' capabilities to act professionally and to control territory without antagonizing the population. Our document reviews and interviews indicated that planners and implementers often failed to understand these important linkages between DIB objectives and other U.S. objectives.

Even more challenging than understanding the linkages among objectives or the best practices discussed above are significant structural constraints that inhibit the United States from effectively applying SSR and DIB lessons. Although we focused our recommendations primarily on small, concrete steps that DoD officials can implement relatively quickly and easily, we recognize a larger need to address problems like insufficient resources and legislative constraints that impede comprehensive, multiyear approaches.

We recommend OSD and AFRICOM jointly develop a DIB best practices briefing tailored to Africa for use by AFRICOM staff, U.S. embassy country team officials, and other stakeholders. This briefing could address both strategic guidance—highlighting the central role of DIB in accomplishing U.S. defense objectives in Africa—as well as lessons from past institutional reform efforts. Joint development of such a briefing would also help align how OSD and AFRICOM staff understand and discuss DIB.

More broadly, we recommend DoD leaders work with Congress to address the need for additional DIB-related resources (for DoD as well as other agencies) and to facilitate whole-of-government, long-term DIB efforts.

Findings and Recommendations from Our Review of DIB Programs in Africa

Our review of DoD documents and interviews highlighted the particular challenges of planning and executing DIB programs in Africa, and the complex relationship of such programs with other security cooperation efforts. OSD and AFRICOM officials disagreed on DIB priorities and even the definition of DIB. In part because of different understandings of DIB and in part because DoD planners did not consistently document activities, monitoring of activities was uneven. Coordination challenges among OSD, AFRICOM, and other stakeholders led to ineffective articulation of requirements. The disconnects among OSD, AFRICOM, U.S. embassy country team officials, and DIB program managers and implementers created two significant problems for African partners. First, communicating DIB opportunities to African partners and understanding partner interests was often poorly executed. In one case, funds allocated for an AMEP activity had to be reallocated to other country accounts after the partner failed to respond. Second, several interviewees stated that African partners did not always get the substantive or regional expertise required for an effective partnership.

Our review of security cooperation programs relevant to DIB in Africa found that there are more DIB-related programs than is generally thought. We identified 47 U.S. government programs that can be leveraged to address specific DIB requirements. DIB programs like MoDA and WIF have expanded their geographic reach, while relatively new programs like the SGI and AMEP are focused on Africa. DIB can be implemented through a variety of activities, including sending of advisors, needs assessments, education, information exchanges, and personnel exchanges. With 22 education programs available for African partners, there are especially promising DIB opportunities in this area. While navigating such a large and varied array of programs can be challenging, it provides options for implementing DIB in ways that may be more palatable to sensitive partners—for example, offering an exchange of personnel to a partner nation reluctant to host a U.S. advisor. Thus, strengthening DIB efforts in Africa does not require creating new programs but rather focusing existing programs in this direction. For example, the National Guard's SPP could increase the number of partnerships in Africa and focus engagements on DIB.

Based on these reviews, we recommend AFRICOM develop a security cooperation playbook with a prominent section on DIB. This playbook would be written in simple language describing how DIB supports other U.S. objectives and how it can be used with African partners. It could help planners and implementers coordinate activities internally and communicate with African partners. For example, RAND research has found that U.S. Northern Command effectively uses playbooks to facilitate DoD support to U.S. disaster response efforts.[1] Easily accessible, informal guidance can help translate official directives for implementers and make execution of complex activities with multiple stakeholders more effective.

Our research also found that developing the right mix of programs and integrating them into a comprehensive, sustainable DIB effort that also supports overall security cooperation goals, requires extensive training. Despite some progress in this area, our analysis found that current training for DIB planners and implementers remains insufficient and somewhat ad hoc. Thus, we also recommend OSD, DSCA, and AFRICOM collaborate to institute improved DIB training. This could be accomplished in two ways. First DSCA's Defense Institute of Security Assistance Management could add a DIB familiarization module (in-residence and online) as part of its training for relevant U.S. officials, and the Institute's regional coordinator for AFRICOM could tailor a component of the module specifically for implementing DIB in Africa. Second, AFRICOM could institutionalize DIB training in-house and integrate it with other security cooperation training it conducts for its staff.

Given the challenges that AFRICOM and U.S. embassy country team personnel face in integrating the planning across DIB and other security cooperation efforts, we recommend AFRICOM develop guid-

---

[1]   Michael J. McNerney, Christopher M. Schnaubelt, Agnes Gereben Schaefer, Martina Melliand, and Bill Gelfeld, *Improving DoD Support to FEMA's All-Hazards Plans*, Santa Monica, Calif.: RAND Corporation, RR-1301-OSD, 2015.

ance for country desk officers to consistently coordinate DIB planning efforts across the command and country teams. This would help harmonize DIB-related objectives in country-level plans, such as AFRICOM's CCPs and the State Department's ICSs

We also found opportunities to strengthen coordination within the U.S. government by improving DoD organizational structures and relationships in three ways. First, we recommend AFRICOM strengthen the DIB coordinator office and institutionalize an annual DIB conference (perhaps in concert with an annual security cooperation conference). Second, we recommend that DSCA take full responsibility for DIB program management and play a greater role integrating DIB with the full range of U.S. government security cooperation activities. Third, we recommend that OSD set up a DIB enterprise liaison at AFRICOM as part of AFRICOM's DIB coordinator office. Ideally, this liaison could come from a central DIB enterprise organization that coordinates DIB across all of DoD and reports to DoD's DIB Coordination Board.[2]

Finally, our review of DIB programs in Africa also included an analysis of whether a more structured approach to prioritizing partner countries could improve how planners select partners and how they determine what types of DIB activities particular countries should receive. Despite their limitations, we found that planners could use an approach like the one we describe in Chapter Three to complement existing efforts to assess and prioritize partners and types of DIB. We recommend OSD and AFRICOM review our country analysis based on the IIAG and consider incorporating similar analysis into their DIB decisionmaking processes.

---

[2] The DIB enterprise concept is described in Perry et al., forthcoming. The DIB Coordination Board will be established upon approval of DoD Directive 5205.JB, *Defense Institution Building* (Under Secretary of Defense for Policy, 2015).

Findings and Recommendations from Liberia and Libya Case Studies

We used case studies of DIB planning in Liberia and Libya to help analyze how DIB goals were established and linked to broader objectives and other security cooperation activities, and—for Liberia—how planners implemented and assessed DIB activities.

In Liberia, we identified several best practices. First, effective planning was closely tied to effective coordination mechanisms both within Liberia and back to planners in AFRICOM and Washington, D.C. Second, DIB effectiveness required long time horizons and strong relationship-building, for example, through a U.S. defense advisor embedded at the Liberian MoD and through U.S. mentors in country for six- to 12-month rotations. Third, implementation benefited from linking DIB to partner nation objectives and thereby ensuring partner commitment. We also identified persistent challenges, such as inconsistent partner involvement, weak partner absorptive capacity, lack of a common operating picture among security cooperation planners, and ad hoc assessment efforts.

In Libya, we identified several lessons relevant for DIB in Africa as a whole. First, DIB planning benefits from a comprehensive strategy informed by a robust baseline assessment. In the case of Libya, the DIRI program was designated to perform this role. Although the security environment stalled the effort, planners at every level agreed on the value of designating a team to provide such an assessment. Second, a comprehensive DIB strategy sets the stage for a common approach based on a common understanding of challenges, objectives, and measure of effectiveness. Third, coordination among diverse stakeholders is possible even in the most challenging environments. DoD coordination with UN officials was effective both on the ground and at the headquarters level. There was room for improvement, however, in terms of OSD doing more to provide insights on DIB-related capabilities and AFRICOM doing more to provide insights on country-level requirements. Fourth, DIB presents particular challenges in post-conflict or less stable environments. Generally, the partner nation's ability and willingness to engage should weigh heavily in decisions about DIB investments. There may be policy reasons, however, to risk resources in especially fragile countries, and an overly cautious approach may limit the ability to effectively engage when an opportunity arises.

We recommend OSD organize a pilot effort in a single African country to serve as a model for future DIB activities. An integrated planning team composed of officials from OSD, the State Department, NSC staff, DSCA, AFRICOM, partner nation decisionmakers, and international partners could produce a five-year DIB plan. The plan would be based on a comprehensive baseline assessment conducted jointly with partner nation and international officials and with inputs from civil society organizations. Implementation would leverage several of the 47 programs we identified in Chapter Three and include a senior advisor deployed for one to three years to help coordinate the effort and build relationships with the partner nation and international partners on the ground. DoD could also leverage the Army's Regionally Aligned Force for Africa, a National Guard state partner, or other units to build relationships and provide continuity.

Findings from Analysis of AFRICOM Assessment Process, Regional Centers, and U.S. Allies

In this report's appendixes, we describe our insights from three additional areas of research. First, we analyzed AFRICOM's assessment process. Second, we looked at how DoD's regional centers function as DIB providers. Third, we drew lessons from the experiences of two U.S. allies active in Africa: France and the United Kingdom.

Our review of AFRICOM's assessment process highlighted significant challenges for DIB. AFRICOM's 2012 TCP established multiple levels of objectives and assessed progress against the relatively more specific IMOs. Because AFRICOM had no IMOs relating to DIB, these activities were not assessed. The impact of DIB, and security cooperation activities more generally, is difficult to quantify, but assessment methods do exist. Previous RAND research has explored security cooperation assessment methods in some detail.[3] Despite the challenges, if DIB in Africa is to be assessed, we recommend that AFRICOM establish one or more IMOs for it.

Our review of DoD's regional centers illustrated the potential value of what we call Type 2 DIB (defense professionalization), but we also found a surprising degree of disagreement and confusion about the centers' role in advancing DIB objectives. We recommend that, as OSD, AFRICOM, and DSCA develop the DIB best practices briefing, DIB playbook, and improved training we suggested earlier in this chapter, they include guidance that describes the desired role of regional centers and other Type 2 DIB programs. In addition to helping link regional center activities to DIB goals, such guidance could help regional centers develop new activities and help OSD and AFRICOM officials prioritize regional center activities against the activities of other DIB-related programs, based on their respective strengths.

Our review of France's decades-long effort to strengthen African defense institutions highlighted several best practices in the following areas:

- adapt the type and level of DIB effort to the partner nation
- obtain partner nation validation at every stage
- develop a good understanding of the institutional structure and political dynamics of the partner nation
- monitor projects closely
- apply multiyear time horizons
- coordinate DIB efforts with other countries to reduce costs and increase impact.

---

[3] McNerney et al., 2014; Jennifer D. P. Moroney, Beth Grill, Joe Hogler, Lianne Kennedy-Boudali, and Christopher Paul, *How Successful Are U.S. Efforts to Build Capacity in Developing Countries? A Framework to Assess the Global Train and Equip "1206" Program*, Santa Monica, Calif.: RAND Corporation, TR-1121-OSD, 2011; Jennifer D. P. Moroney Joe Hogler, Jefferson P. Marquis, Christopher Paul, John E. Peters, and Beth Grill, *Developing an Assessment Framework for U.S. Air Force Building Partnerships Programs*, Santa Monica, Calif.: RAND Corporation, MG-868-AF, 2010; Christopher Paul, Jessica Yeats, Colin P. Clarke, Miriam Matthews, and Lauren Skrabala, *Assessing and Evaluating Department of Defense Efforts to Inform, Influence, and Persuade: Handbook for Practitioners*, Santa Monica, Calif.: RAND Corporation, RR-809/2-OSD, 2015.

We recommend OSD and AFRICOM staff discuss with French officials opportunities to participate in France's 16 regional defense schools across Africa, which have proved successful at building relationships and strengthening African institutions through PME.

As with our review of French experiences, the UK's engagement in DIB activities highlights several best practices:

- assessments should focus on local citizen perceptions of institutions
- ambitions should match resources
- DIB requires a whole-of-government approach
- working with allies can enhance impact
- political and cultural awareness about the partner nation is crucial.

Although UK DIB investments are low, we recommend OSD and AFRICOM staff coordinate more closely with UK officials on DIB efforts in Africa—particularly the north and west. In particular, there may be opportunities to create hubs for DIB knowledge sharing at select DoD sites and at one or more of France's regional defense schools in Africa.

Conclusion

For the reasons described in this report, planning and implementing DIB effectively in Africa is particularly challenging. Nevertheless, we have identified several ways to strengthen links between DIB planning and the wider range of country planning and U.S. defense objectives in Africa. Without these improvements, we argue that not only will DIB objectives be put at risk, but broader U.S. defense objectives in Africa as well.

Because it requires different skills than most operationally and tactically focused engagements, effective DIB requires particularly close coordination between OSD and combatant commands. Intensive involvement by other stakeholders (DSCA, U.S. embassy country team officials, partner nation officials, U.S. allies, etc.) is also crucial. Through the steps above, and other actions discussed in the report, coordination should improve, along with the ability to enable DIB to advance U.S. defense objectives in Africa.

AFRICOM Assessment Process

As is the case with the other combatant commands, AFRICOM has developed its own methodology to evaluate whether DIB activities are creating the intended effects. However, with AFRICOM being a relatively young command (established in 2007), its assessment process is less developed than the processes at the other major commands.

AFRICOM's assessment process is conducted by the J8 Assessment Division and, as in the other commands, it is based on TCP guidance.[1] The J5 is tasked with the coordination of all assessment criteria between each U.S. embassy country team, the SDO, and the DATT. The J5 also provides AFRICOM assessment requirements to support Africa Contingency Operations Training and Assistance (ACOTA) programs.

Finally, the J5 maintains an online security cooperation database as a data source for steady-state assessments.[2] Like other commands, AFRICOM tracks security assistance (including DIB) activities using DoD's Theater Security Cooperation Management Information System.

The basic elements affecting the assessment process in the 2012 AFRICOM TCP are depicted in Figure A.1.

---

[1] Please see footnote 40 on p. 49 for updated TCP information.

[2] Commander, U.S. Africa Command, *AFRICOM Theater Campaign, Plan 7000-12*, January 25, 2012, pp. 30–32.

Figure A.1
FY 2012–2016 AFRICOM Planning and Assessment Process

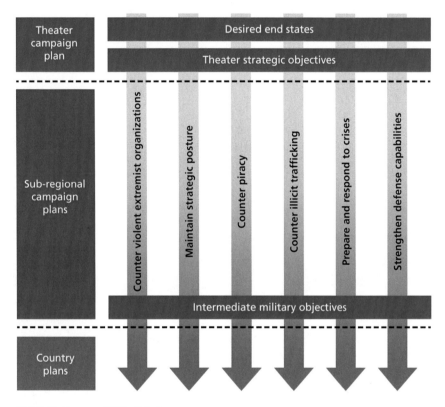

SOURCE: Hooper, 2013, slide 6.
RAND RR1232-A.1

The major components were as follows:[3]

- **Theater strategic objectives:** From end states identified in higher-level DoD planning guidance, the AFRICOM TCP developed its own tailored objectives known as "theater strategic objectives," or TSOs.

---

[3]   Commander, U.S. Africa Command, 2012, pp. 24–26; Commander, U.S. Africa Command, *AFRICOM Theater Campaign, Plan 7000-10*, January 25, 2010.

- **Lines of effort:** AFRICOM established six LOEs that aligned with the command's theater strategic objectives.[4]
- **Intermediate military objectives:** AFRICOM developed IMOs aimed at supporting the LOEs. The annual assessment process was aimed at gauging how well the command had progressed toward achieving the IMOs.
- **Country-level objectives:** Country-level objectives were developed within *individual* country plans so that guidance may be implemented and achieved at the country level.

AFRICOM's FY 2012 TCP listed six distinct LOEs that tied in to AFRICOMs theater security objectives.[5] These appear in the vertical arrows of Figure A.1. AFRICOM listed the following LOEs in its TCP, each having the flexibility to be tailored to a specific country (i.e., at the country plan level).

- counter violent extremist organizations
- maintain strategic posture
- counter piracy
- counter illicit trafficking
- prepare and respond to crises
- strengthening defense capabilities.

Strengthening defense capabilities was the only LOE related to achieving DIB objectives, and some officials stated it had the lowest priority.[6] The focus of this LOE was to "improve partners' generating forces, specifically their institutional systems, in order to produce professional, effective operational forces."[7]

---

[4] The FY 2016–2020 TCP reflected multiple changes to IMOs, LOEs, and their related assessments. Please see footnote 40 on page 49.

[5] Commander, U.S. Africa Command, 2012, pp. 24–26.

[6] Interviews with DoD officials, April and October 2014. Some AFRICOM planners were "not sure that the six LOEs were ever prioritized."

[7] Commander, U.S. Africa Command, 2012, pp. 24–26.

The assessment process, conducted by the J8, measured the degree to which the IMOs had been achieved during the assessment cycle. As in other commands, the IMOs were the foundation for assessments and, as such, they had to be specific and measurable. IMOs provided the basis for assessing progress toward desired AFRICOM end-states and also informed AFRICOM priorities (levels of effort) and future resource allocation for the command.

Several IMOs in support of the strengthening defense capabilities LOE described the intended effects of security cooperation and assessed progress against them, but there were no IMOs that addressed DIB directly. Some of the IMOs described effects that were relevant to DIB, but only indirectly. The IMOs intended effects relied on objective indicators and therefore could not take subjective assessments into account, which are crucial to the DIB process. The assessments process was also complicated by rapidly evolving events on the ground that may have negated previous baseline assessments conducted by country teams.

DoD's Regional Centers as DIB Providers

Two DoD regional centers for security studies develop capacity-building academic programs for African countries. The Africa Center for Strategic Studies (ACSS) works with all 54 countries on the African continent save Egypt, while the Near East and South Asia Center for Strategic Studies (NESA) works with the countries of the Maghreb. Both contribute to DIB objectives on the continent, though they do so through broad, strategic-level educational programs rather than through hands-on operational training initiatives like those undertaken by DIRI, DIILS, and MoDA. As a result, their direct impact on DIB objectives is harder to measure.

Background

The five DoD regional centers for security studies are key tools for building strategic capacity among partner nation security establishments. The centers work to advance policy priorities stated by the OSD and security cooperation objectives identified by the regional combatant commands.

The centers have been charged with strengthening partner nations' defense institutions for at least a decade. The centers' DIB mission was defined by the Secretary of Defense and reaffirmed multiple times in policy guidance from senior OSD officials.

- DoD Directive 5200.41, signed by the Secretary of Defense in 2004, states, "A core Regional Center mission shall be to support the Department's policies and priorities by assisting military and civilian leaders in the region in developing strong defense establishments and strengthening civil-military relations in a democratic society."[1]

- In January 2008, Under Secretary of Defense for Policy Eric S. Edelman produced a three-page document entitled "Policy Guidance to the DoD Regional Centers." Among the "core tasks" assigned to the centers was a directive to "[b]uild capacity of partners' national security institutions consistent with the norms of civil-military relations." The guidance also stated that one of the centers' goals was to promote "improved sustainable institutional capacity to enhance national, regional, and international security."[2]

- To provide the centers with concrete direction on how to implement the January 2008 Edelman guidance, the following month Assistant Secretary of Defense for International Security Affairs Joseph Benkert issued a memo on policy priorities for the regional centers, in which he wrote that the regional centers "are key to DoD efforts to build partner institutional capacity."[3]

- Updated policy guidance from Under Secretary of Defense for Policy Michèle Flournoy issued in February 2011 reiterated the key elements of the Edelman memo, including the mission of strengthening partners' institutional capacity. However, Flournoy also directed the centers to emphasize whole-of-government solutions to complex security challenges, an approach that included collaboration between civilian and military institutions, the pro-

---

[1]   Under Secretary of Defense for Policy, *DoD Centers for Regional Security Studies*, Department of Defense Directive 5200.41, July 30, 2004 (certified current as of December 5, 2008), para 3.1. See also Larry Hanauer, Stuart E. Johnson, Christopher J. Springer, Chaoling Feng, Michael J. McNerney, Stephanie Pezard, and Shira Efron, *Evaluating the Impact of the Department of Defense Regional Centers for Security Studies*, Santa Monica, Calif.: RAND Corporation, RR-388-OSD, 2014, pp. 20–21.

[2]   Hanauer et al., 2014, p. 27.

[3]   Joseph Benkert, Assistant Secretary of Defense, "Policy Priorities for DoD Regional Centers Program Planning, 2010–2015," memorandum to the directors of DSCA and the regional centers, February 1, 2008.

motion of democratic accountability, respect for human rights, and the rule of law.[4]

The centers conduct a wide range of activities to promote the policy objectives defined by OSD Policy. Their core academic programs consist of resident executive development seminars and non-resident workshops that are typically held in-region. The centers also engage in research on issues of interest to U.S. and regional policymakers and undertake robust alumni outreach efforts, which include some alumni-focused academic programs.[5]

According to ACSS, almost all of its academic programs and initiatives advance AFRICOM's DIB objectives. In its FY 2014 program plan, ACSS proposed 12 academic courses; one program would be offered twice and another (its regional workshop series) would be offered 11 times, yielding a total of 23 classroom programs. In addition, ACSS's plan describes two supporting efforts: academic research and strategic outreach, which consists primarily of senior-level visits, exchanges, and meetings. The program plan specifies whether each program provides "significant focus" or "indirect support" to OSD's priorities for the regional center enterprise, OSD's policy priorities for Africa, and AFRICOMs FY 2012 TCP LOEs. The document indicates that 19 of ACSS's 23 proposed classroom programs, plus its research and outreach, place a "significant focus" on AFRICOM's strengthen defense institutions LOE. In addition, two programs provide "indirect support" to this DIB-focused LOE. Only one program—its introduction to African security issues course, which it proposed offering twice during the year—was marked as not advancing AFRICOM's DIB LOE at all.[6] NESA's planning documents, which provide far less detail, do not reference the extent to which the center's programs promote institution building, though they do assert that NESA programs

---

[4]   Michèle Flournoy, Under Secretary of Defense, "Policy Guidance for the Department of Defense (DoD) Regional Centers," memorandum to regional center directors, February 28, 2011.

[5]   DSCA, *Regional Centers for Security Studies: FY2011 Annual Report*, undated, p. 2.

[6]   Africa Center for Strategic Studies, *FY2014 Program Plan*, December 12, 2013.

"support political and economic reform in the Middle East and North Africa" and include "strategic capacity building initiatives" that address "the role of defense in civil society," phrases that, taken together, refer broadly to similar objectives.[7]

Comparison Between the Regional Centers and Other DIB Programs

Although ACSS and NESA undertake programs that address institution building, they fill a different niche in U.S. security cooperation engagement than other DIB programs. An April 2014 RAND assessment of the effectiveness of the regional center enterprise noted the following distinctions between the centers and DIB programs like DIRI and DIILS.

The centers emphasize broad, strategic analysis of regional security challenges with an emphasis on whole-of-government policy solutions. Other DIB programs, such as DIRI and DIILS, focus on examining narrow subject areas in a country-specific context with an emphasis on implementing concrete solutions in collaboration with partners in the defense sector. Also, whereas the regional centers interact extensively with alumni in partner nations over time, other DIB programs engage periodically with a small group of officials and undertake few, if any, outreach efforts to program alumni.[8] The uniqueness of the regional centers is summarized in Table B.1.

Regional Centers' Strengths and Weaknesses as DIB Tools

ACSS and NESA, without question, shape bilateral defense relations in ways that facilitate discussion of DIB-related issues and pave the way for DoD DIB-focused programs to engage partner nations. That said,

---

[7]   Near East and South Asia Center for Strategic Studies, unpublished FY2013-2014 Program Plan, May 11, 2012.

[8]   Hanauer, et al., p. 132.

Table B.1
Comparison of the Regional Centers and DIB Programs (DIILS, DIRI, MoDA)

Regional Centers	DIB Programs
Emphasis on policy	Emphasis on implementation
Multidisciplinary analysis	Deep dive on specific topic
Regionally focused	Global scope, country-specific application
Interagency participation	MoD/military participation
Whole-of-government solutions	Defense-focused solutions
Build regional relationships	Build bilateral relationships
Continuous engagement throughout the areas of responsibility	Periodic extended engagement with individual countries
Frequent alumni outreach	Limited to no alumni outreach

SOURCE: Hanauer et al., 2014, p. 132.

it is difficult to identify (much less quantify) the precise ways in which the centers contribute to DIB objectives, which leads AFRICOM officials to express a preference for using DIRI, DIILS, and other DIB-specific programs to advance the command's DIB goals.[9]

Laying the Groundwork for Other DIB Programs

Although regional center staff do not sit alongside partner nation officials in country-specific, hands-on efforts to design and implement institutional reforms, the centers' strategically focused academic programs help promote acceptance of DIB concepts among senior (and soon-to-be senior) partner nation officials, thereby setting the stage for more "traditional" DIB programs to work with partners to implement defense reforms. The regional centers train a small number of potential movers and shakers who can drive institution building and reform from a senior level; DIB programs train a larger number of mid-level officials to build a constituency for institution building, develop operational plans for reform in partnership with host nation officials, and

---

[9] Telephone interview with AFRICOM official, September 9, 2014.

generate positive long-term momentum. Neither the academic nor the hands-on approach is necessarily better than the other. Indeed, AFRI-COM officials assert that both types of engagement are needed over time.[10]

Regional Centers Allow Persistent Engagement on DIB

DIRI, DIILS, and MoDA engage a small number of specific countries for limited periods, which enables intense, short-term collaboration on institution building. The corollary of this focus, however, is that most countries receive little or no DIB-focused training from these programs for many years.

In contrast, ACSS and NESA engage small numbers of officials from throughout their focus regions on an ongoing basis. As "steady state engagement tools," the regional centers are positioned to maintain a dialogue on institution building in the absence of other security cooperation engagements or despite the waxing and waning of bilateral relations with the United States.[11] The centers' active engagement with their alumni—something other DIB programs do not do—enhances their ability to maintain dialogues with partners over the long term.[12]

Regional Centers Open Doors to DIB, but Others May Be Better Suited to Walk Through

ACSS and NESA are particularly well suited to engage on DIB topics in countries with limited military-to-military ties with the United States, either because relations have never been close or because previously productive ties have become strained.

Some African partners—particularly those with little experience working with U.S. military counterparts—are wary of engaging the U.S. military. In such countries, an AFRICOM official stated, host nation leaders may be suspicious of a U.S. military advisor working

---

[10] Telephone interview with AFRICOM official, September 9, 2014; telephone interview with AFRICOM official, September 17, 2014.

[11] Hanauer et al., 2014, p. 90.

[12] Interview with NESA officials, August 13, 2014. Also interview with ACSS officials, August 26, 2014 (Interview L1).

inside the ministry through the MoDA program or of a U.S. military DIRI team that arrives to write new policies and regulations. In contrast, a U.S. offer to send partner officers to ACSS or another PME program is less intrusive and may thus be viewed with less suspicion. This "lighter touch" enables regional centers to promote U.S. defense reform and institution building goals in countries where other programs may be seen as suspect.[13]

Indeed, "the regional centers," according to the January 2008 Edelman guidance, "are vital instruments for cultivating new and existing partnerships."[14] One of the principal roles of the regional centers, the Edelman memo states, is to build and maintain relations with partner nation officials on a wide range of topics. As one AFRICOM official put it, ACSS and NESA are very good at "opening doors to dialogue" by engaging partner officials at a strategic level, particularly in countries where AFRICOM has minimal engagement and a limited footprint. He added, however, that others—DIRI, MoDA, and combatant command staff—are better suited to walk through those doors and engage in dialogues on DIB-specific goals because these other entities have more tools at their disposal to address them in concrete ways.[15]

ACSS and NESA staff disagree, arguing that their in-depth regional expertise enables them to address DIB in a more appropriate cultural context. The centers' permanent staff, ACSS and NESA officials asserted, possess in-depth regional expertise that enables them to tailor institution-building programs to the local context; in contrast, the DIB programs, regional center staff stated, hire functional experts on contract who apply a standard model to DIB tasks (such as defense strategy writing) without regard to whether it is well suited to the specific partner nation.[16] There are likely benefits to applying both

---

[13] Telephone interview with AFRICOM official, September 17, 2014.

[14] Eric S. Edelman, Under Secretary of Defense for Policy, "Policy Guidance for the DOD Regional Centers," memorandum, January 18, 2008.

[15] Telephone interview with AFRICOM official, September 9, 2014.

[16] Interview with NESA officials, August 13, 2014; interview with ACSS officials, August 26, 2014.

regional and functional expertise to DIB challenges, no matter which U.S. entity may be leading the engagement.

Previous RAND research reported that regional centers are valuable tools for engaging countries when broader bilateral military relationships are strained or have been suspended, perhaps because a coup, internal instability, U.S. sanctions, or political tensions have prevented senior-level dialogues or ongoing security cooperation.[17] In such cases, few (if any) partner nation officials attend U.S. PME courses through IMET, and DIB programs typically allocate their resources to other countries. ACSS and NESA, however, are authorized to continue engaging officials from countries even as other DoD programs pull back. In such cases, ACSS and NESA can serve as the only means of addressing U.S. DIB objectives. As an example, ACSS was recently asked to hold a bilateral event with the interim regime in the Central African Republic, which had been cut off from military assistance since rebels deposed the government in early 2013.

Effect of Regional Centers on DIB Exists but Is Difficult to Quantify

Previous RAND research found a widespread belief among OSD and combatant command officials that the regional center enterprise does indeed help partner nations build and manage their defense and security institutions.[18] Moreover, these officials stated, other DIB initiatives are more effective because of the foundational institution building work done by the regional centers.[19]

That said, AFRICOM officials point out that ACSS and NESA contribute to the command's DIB objectives only indirectly, principally by facilitating dialogues with partner nation officials that address DIB and other topics.[20] One AFRICOM official noted that while ACSS's and NESA's academic approach to DIB was broadly useful, the centers cannot demonstrate how their programs have directly advanced the

---

[17] Hanauer et al., 2014, pp. 88–91.

[18] Hanauer et al., 2014, p. 29.

[19] Hanauer et al., 2014, p. 80.

[20] Telephone interview with AFRICOM official, September 9, 2014.

command's DIB objectives; whereas ACSS and NESA discuss institution building, programs like DIRI and DIILS actually tackle DIB-related challenges.[21]

Regional Centers Are Not Considered in AFRICOM DIB Planning

DIB is one of six LOEs in the 2012 AFRICOM TCP and is therefore a significant focus for the command's regional security cooperation engagement.[22] However, because the regional centers' impact on DIB objectives is seen as somewhat impalpable, AFRICOM staff assert that the command emphasizes the use of DIB programs when developing its engagement plans. One AFRICOM official asserted that ACSS and NESA do not factor into the command's plans because they are not "operationally relevant."[23] This dynamic stands in stark contrast to ACSS's own presentation of its programs, the majority of which the center claimed related directly to AFRICOM's DIB LOE.

Summary

While AFRICOM officials acknowledge that the regional centers' academic programs help advance DIB goals in a broad sense, they see more palpable benefit in programs like DIRI and DIILS that work to implement defense reforms. These programs, AFRICOM officials asserted, make more substantial and visible contributions to the concrete DIB goals that are outlined in the DIB LOE of the command's TCP. In essence, AFRICOM officials see clearer value in hands-on, results-driven training programs such as DIRI and DIILS than in the broader educational programs undertaken by the regional centers.

If ACSS and NESA are to contribute to DIB objectives in Africa, they should make the linkages between their programs and AFRICOM's DIB goals clearer and more explicit, and they should work with AFRICOM staff to determine whether new or existing programs—

---

[21] Telephone interview with AFRICOM official, September 9, 2014.

[22] Please see footnote 40 on p. 49 for updated TCP information.

[23] Telephone interview with AFRICOM official, September 9, 2014.

perhaps funded with AFRICOM funds—could more directly address the command's priorities.

It may also be valuable for a higher-level DoD entity, such as OSD or AFRICOM, to provide strategic guidance to the entire DIB enterprise. Such guidance could ensure that DIB initiatives undertaken by the regional centers, DIRI, DIILS, MoDA, and other programs advance the same goals while also clarifying each program's specific missions and assigning priorities to each that draws on their respective strengths. The DoD Inspector General recommended such a broader policy on DIB initiatives in a November 2012 report on the DIRI program, writing

> Without DIB policy that distinguished the DIB roles of the DIRI Program and the Regional Centers or any other office or command conducting DIB-related efforts, a potential for duplication and inefficiency existed.[24]

---

[24] Office of the Inspector General, *Defense Institution Reform Initiative Program Elements Need to Be Defined*, Washington, D.C.: Department of Defense, DODIG-2013-019, November 9, 2012, p. 13.

Allied Experience in DIB

U.S. experience in DIB is not as deep as some other countries. Two with substantial experience in DIB or DIB-like efforts are close allies—France and the United Kingdom. This appendix describes their experiences in Africa, how that experience fits with other security cooperation efforts sponsored by their respective countries, and what lessons the United States might draw from those experiences.

France

Overview

Although they may not call them "DIB," U.S. allies have also been conducting similar types of activities with their respective partner countries. France, for instance, has kept a dense network of relationships with African countries and undertakes DIB activities as part of its "structural cooperation" missions through PME and advisory work. Although less involved in Africa than France and the United States, the UK (for whom DIB falls under "Defence Diplomacy") has taken part in the reform of the defense sector in, mainly, Sierra Leone, Nigeria, and Ghana. Both countries have met some challenges and are in the process of dealing with them to improve the efficiency of their DIB missions. France is putting together a more stringent system for requests and assessments that should help it focus its efforts where it serves France's strategic interests best. The UK is examining whether its ambitions match the resources it devotes to DIB. Both countries have also gathered lessons from their extensive experience of DIB in Africa, some of which may be relevant for U.S. activities. Lessons from France include adapting the type and level of DIB effort to the partner nation; obtaining partner nation validation at every stage; knowing well the institutions of the partner nation; monitoring DIB projects closely; being patient; and coordinating with other organizations providing assistance to deliver the best DIB programs at the lowest cost. The UK has shared some of these same lessons. Additional insights from the UK experience include matching ambitions to resources, promoting a whole-of-government approach on the British side, and focusing on local perceptions of institutions as measures of effectiveness of DIB efforts.

Introduction

France maintains strong security relations with a large number of African countries, particularly in francophone areas. These relations take the form of a flurry of security cooperation activities, categorized as structural or operational cooperation depending on the type of activities and the relevant agency. France engages in DIB—one element of structural cooperation—through two main tools: PME (both in France and in Africa) and advisory work. It has also developed an original PME model through the regionally oriented national schools (*écoles nationales à vocation régionale*, ENVR), which offer high-quality curricula to students of a same region. France also sends advisors to work closely with high-level officials, as well as small teams of experts that perform audits of various defense institutions for partner nations.

France has recently revised some of its processes to solicit requests for cooperation from partner nations, and to assess progress on ongoing projects. These changes reflect an ambition to be more effective, promote a tighter strategic focus, and ensure that cooperation programs play a role in actually building partner nations' institutions rather than simply sustain French presence in these countries.

This appendix first examines France's strategic interests in Africa before turning to the key categories and processes that underpin security cooperation. It then analyzes how France prioritizes partner nations, assesses the projects it carries out with them, and works with other DIB providers. A conclusion highlights insights from the French experience and offers recommendations on their potential implications for DoD.

France's Strategic Interests in Africa

Following decolonization in the 1960s, France has kept close military ties with most francophone countries. In some cases, it signed defense agreements with its former colonies that offered the guarantee of French military support in case of a coup, external aggression, or aggression by state-sponsored rebel groups. These agreements were revised following former French President Nicolas Sarkozy's February 2008 speech in South Africa announcing a new French policy in Africa, and France's military intervention is now by no means automatic.[1] Still, resorting to military intervention to safeguard its national interests in Africa remains in France's realm of potential policy choices, as the 2012 intervention in Mali (Operation Serval) and the 2013 intervention in Central African Republic (Operation Sangaris) made clear.

France has key strategic interests on the African continent that explain the continuation of these relationships. These interests include strong economic relationships and the necessity to guarantee the safety of its many nationals living in Africa. Senegal, Côte d'Ivoire, Gabon, Madagascar, and Réunion Island each host more than 10,000 French nationals.[2] Mali, the Republic of Congo, Cameroon, Djibouti, and South Africa have 4,800 to 10,000 French nationals each.[3] France's key defense guidance document, the April 2013 White Paper on Defense (*Livre Blanc de la Défense*),[4] makes it a key strategic priority for France to stabilize Europe's surroundings—including Northern and, increasingly, Western Africa—with partners and allies.[5]

As a result, France has established an extensive military and diplomatic presence in Africa. Aside from the United States in Djibouti,

---

[1] André Dulait, Robert Hue, Yves Pozzo di Borgo, and Didier Boulaud, "La France et la gestion des crises africaines: quels changements possibles?" French Senate, Committee on Foreign Affairs, Information Report No. 405 (2005–2006), July 3, 2006.

[2] Réunion Island is one of France's Overseas Departments (*départements d'Outre-Mer*).

[3] As of June 2013. Jeanny Lorgeoux and Jean-Marie Bockel, "L'Afrique est notre avenir," French Senate, Committee on Foreign Affairs, Defence and Armed Forces, Information Report No. 104 (2013–2014), October 29, 2013.

[4] Hereafter referred to as the "White Paper on Defense."

[5] French Ministry of Defense, *Livre Blanc Défense et sécurité nationale [White Paper on Defense and National Security]*, 2013, pp. 47–60.

France is the only Western country with permanent bases in Africa in Gabon, Réunion Island, and Senegal. As of 2014, France had 24 defense or cooperation agreements, mostly with francophone countries in northern, western, and central Africa.[6] According to the White Paper on Defense, the purpose of these 24 agreements is to get African states to "own and master their security" and to give French forces "easier anticipation and reaction" capabilities.[7] To a lesser extent, France is also active outside of its traditional area of influence, with technical arrangements (which only cover specific cooperation activities) or status of forces agreements with countries in eastern (e.g., Kenya) or southern Africa (e.g., Botswana and Malawi).[8]

DIB in the Broader Security Cooperation Architecture

Structural and Operational Cooperation
French security cooperation activities are divided in two categories: structural cooperation, which is run by the Ministry of Foreign Affairs and International Development through the *Direction de la Coopération de Sécurité et de Défense* (DCSD) and operational cooperation, which is run by the MoD through the Joint Staff (*État-Major des Armées*). At the embassy level, the defense attaché is in charge of security cooperation and refers to both the Joint Staff and DCSD.[9]

Structural cooperation includes PME and advisory activities. These activities usually target partner nations' military officers and are carried out by French military *coopérants*, who are trainers or advisors detached from their military service of origin. As of December 31, 2013, France had 278 *coopérants* worldwide, including 229 military, 41

---

[6] French Ministry of Defense, 2013, p. 55; and Marie Recalde, "Autorisant la ratification du traité instituant un partenariat en matière de coopération militaire entre la République française et la République du Sénégal [Authorizing the ratification of the treaty establishing a partnership in the field of military cooperation between the France Republic and the Republic of Senegal]," French National Assembly, Committee on National Defence and Armed Forces, Legislative Report No. 932, April 16, 2013.

[7] French Ministry of Defense, 2013, p. 55.

[8] Recalde, 2013.

[9] Phone conversation with French Ministry of Defense official No. 1, March 2014.

gendarmes, and eight civil protection personnel. Almost 90 percent of these were in Africa.[10]

Operational cooperation, as its name indicates, covers activities that improve operational readiness and are mostly targeted at partner nations' enlisted personnel. Such activities are carried out by training teams called operational instructional detachments (*détachements d' instruction opérationnelle*) and technical instructional detachments (*détachements d' instruction technique*), that deploy for usually brief amounts of time (a few days to a few weeks) to partner countries.[11] Table C.1 summarizes the differences between structural and operational cooperation.

Although they depend on different ministries, the DCSD and the Joint Staff work together closely. The DCSD depends on the Joint Staff for supplying personnel (the *coopérants*) to undertake cooperation activities. The DCSD is always headed by a French military officer, with the position rotating between the army, navy, and air force.[12] Finally, the Joint Staff may be involved in the selection of advisors (although such advisory work is part of structural cooperation), particularly if the foreign official to be advised is in a high-level position. If the president of a partner nation requires an advisor, for instance, not only the Joint Staff but also the Joint Staff of the French Presidency (*État-major particulier du Président de la République*) would play a role in the selection of that advisor.[13]

---

[10] "Répartition des coopérants militaires," *Partenaires Sécurité Défense*, Vol. 274, June 2014, p. 6. The ten African countries with more than ten French *coopérants* each were Benin, Burkina Faso, Côte d'Ivoire, Guinea, Mali, Niger, Senegal, Togo, Cameroon, Congo, Gabon, Chad, Djibouti, Madagscar, and Morocco.

[11] Jennifer D. P. Moroney, Celeste Gventer, Stephanie Pezard, and Laurence Smallman, *Lessons from U.S. Allies in Security Cooperation with Third Countries: The Cases of Australia, France, and the United Kingdom*, Santa Monica, Calif.: RAND Corporation, TR-972-AF, 2011, p. 37.

[12] Phone conversation with French Ministry of Defense official No. 1, March 2014.

[13] Conversations with former French Ministry of Defense official No. 1, March and May 2014.

Table C.1
Structural and Operational Cooperation

	Structural Cooperation	Operational Cooperation
Relevant authority	Ministry of Foreign Affairs and International Development	Ministry of Defense
Relevant agency	DCSD	Joint Staff
Level	Strategic and operational	Operational only
Time horizon	Long	Short
Type of activities	Education, advice, training	Training, equipment
Examples	Course at the French War School; sending of a ministerial advisor	Exercises; pre-deployment preparation and training
Implementers/trainers	Officers	Enlisted personnel
Audience/trainees	Officers; individuals or organizations	Enlisted personnel; mostly units

SOURCES: Conversations with former French Ministry of Defense official No. 1, March and May 2014; phone conversation with Foreign Affairs and International Development No. 1, July 2014.

How France Defines DIB

DIB does not exist as a separate category within French security cooperation. It is included in structural cooperation and, as such, it falls under the purview of the Ministry of Foreign Affairs and International Development, through the DCSD. Rather than "institution building," the French would describe this type of activity as capacity building at the politico-military or strategic level (*renforcement des capacités au niveau politico-militaire stratégique*).[14] Table C.2 highlights the activities that fit the DoD definition of DIB. PME can fall into either category (DIB or non-DIB) depending on the program's curriculum and target audience.

---

[14] Conversations with former French Ministry of Defense official No. 1, March and May 2014.

DIB Tools and Activities in Africa

This section examines in more detail the two types of DIB activities outlined in Table C.2: PME at the strategic level and expertise (through advisors and small team audits). PME can take place in France or in Africa through a network of ENVRs. Expertise can be provided through advisors who are attached to a given institution or governmental official, or through the sending of small teams that conduct audits or needs assessments. These different types of activities are not mutually exclusive, and some countries may require all three.[15]

Professional Military Education in Africa and in France
ENVRs and French Schools

Starting in 1996, France has been delocalizing part of its PME to Africa by ENVRs. The purpose of these schools is to provide the same education that would be dispensed in France, but at a lesser cost. As an additional benefit, they promote regional integration and cooperation by bringing together students from neighboring nations. A third objective of these schools is to encourage ownership by the partner nations of this project by having them play a key role in the management of the schools. ENVRs cover a large range of topics of various relevance for

Table C.2
French Security Cooperation Activities of Relevance to DIB

	Time Frame	Agency in Charge	Type of Activities	Is It DIB?
Structural cooperation	Long term	DCSD	Technical assistance	No
			PME (technical)	No
			PME (strategic level)	Yes
			Advisors	Yes
			Small team audits	Yes
Operational cooperation	Short term	Joint Staff	Training, exercises, pre-deployment preparation	No

---

[15] Conversations with former French Ministry of Defense official No. 1, March and May 2014.

DIB. Table C.3 lists the 16 existing ENVRs and highlights the ones whose curriculum is closest to DIB.

The ENVR model is a joint venture between France and a partner nation, with an emphasis on the role played by the latter. The partner

Table C.3
Specialties and Locations of the 16 ENVRs

Type of Training	ENVR	Location
General military training	*Advanced Joint Services Defense Course (CSID)*	Yaounde (Cameroon)
	Staff College of Libreville (EEML)	Libreville (Gabon)
	Infantry Officer's Training School (EAI)	Thies (Senegal)
Technical or specialized military training	Construction Engineer School (EGT)	Brazzaville (Congo)
	Regionally Oriented National Aeronautic Centre (PANVR)	Garoua (Cameroon)
	Naval Academy (Navy Training Center)	Bata (Equatorial Guinea)
	Military Engineers College (EMTO)	Ouagadougou (Burkina Faso)
	Military Administration School (EMA)	Koulikoro (Mali)
Military medical training	Military Paramedic Personnel School (EPPAN)	Niamey (Niger)
	Army Medical Corps School (ESSAL)	Lome (Togo)
	Military Medical Practice School (EASSML)	Libreville (Gabon)
Internal security training	*Judicial Police Training Centre (CPPJ)*	Porto-Novo (Benin)
	Law Enforcement Training Centre	Awaé (Cameroon)
	Gendarmerie Officers Training Course (CAOG)	Ouakam (Senegal)
Peacekeeping operations training	Mine Action and Depollution Training Centre (CPADD)	Ouidah (Benin)
	Peacekeeping School (EMP)	Bamako (Mali)

SOURCE: "Les ENVR, une contribution à la paix, la stabilité et la sécurité en Afrique subsaharienne [ENVRs, a contribution to peace, stability and security in Sub-Saharan Africa]," *Partenaires Sécurité Défense*, No. 268, Winter 2012.

NOTE: ENVRs in italics provide some level of DIB training.

nation provides the location, building, and resources (including teaching and administrative staff) for the school, and is in charge of its overall supervision.[16] France provides technical support and expertise by sending two to five *coopérants* who occupy key positions (Director of Studies, for instance) in the faculty or management of the school. France also covers the travel costs for African students, as well as their living expenses and, in some cases, small equipment. Most of ENVRs' faculty comes from the partner nation. In theory, other African countries could provide some teaching staff as well, but the process of detaching one professor from a country to another has proven a major bureaucratic hurdle.[17]

The concept of ENVR has enabled France to create an equivalent in Africa of its own educational institutions. The War College (*École de guerre*) in Paris and the one in Yaoundé, Cameroon, which represent the highest level of education for officers, have the same curriculum.[18] Although primarily aimed at African students, the War College in Yaoundé attracts other nationalities, including French and American students.[19]

Another Africa-centered program is the one-week seminar organized every year by the DCSD and managed by the Institute for Higher National Defense Studies (*Institut de hautes études de défense nationale*, IHEDN) in Paris. This seminar, called the IHEDN Forum on the African Continent (*Forum de l'IHEDN sur le continent africain*), welcomes military and civilian participants who can make a contribution to the annual theme chosen by the DCSD and based on French strategic priorities. In 2014, the theme was maritime security—one of the priority areas defined during the December 2013 Élysée Summit on Africa. Due to budgetary constraints, however, the IHEDN seminar was cut from 15 to nine days. It, too, should soon have its Africa-

---

[16] "Les ENVR, une contribution à la paix . . . ," 2012, p. 11.

[17] Phone conversation with French Ministry of Foreign Affairs and International Development officials No. 2 and No. 3, August 2014.

[18] Conversation with former French Ministry of Defense official No. 2, April 2014.

[19] Phone conversation with French Ministry of Foreign Affairs and International Development officials No. 2 and No. 3, August 2014.

based equivalent. The DCSD was working with the authorities of Côte d'Ivoire to develop a similar course, with a first session planned in 2015.[20]

Limitations of PME

Although PME is an important way to fulfill DIB objectives by educating the next generation of military officers, it has its limitations. One limitation is France's lack of ability to select the students who stand the highest chance of moving onto positions of influence, disseminate what they have learned, and maintain a relationship with France. Generally, partner nations are in charge of that process and pick the students they wish to send to French PME institutions. Several checks exist, however. First, the DATT can provide some input and discuss with the partner nation's Joint Staff if the candidate is grossly inappropriate. The DATT is also the person who has most visibility into the assignment of the student on his or her return to the partner nation.[21] A second check is provided by the test that candidates must take to enter some schools, such as the War College, to make sure they have the prerequisite knowledge to attend the course.[22]

In some cases, the selection process for PME takes the form of a competitive examination. For instance, Senegal organizes a single test to determine which candidates will fill the slots available in various PME institutions (e.g., in France, the United States, Germany, Austria, etc.). The students who score highest on the test get selected, with the first one getting his first choice of school, followed by the second one, and so on. Senegalese authorities do not intervene in this selection process, ensuring that PME slots are offered to the most capable participants rather than given away as a political reward. This process, however, has one major disadvantage, which is that these most-capable participants will not necessarily be the ones who will move onto posi-

---

[20] Phone conversation with French Ministry of Foreign Affairs and International Development officials No. 2 and No. 3, August 2014.

[21] Conversations with former French Ministry of Defense official No. 1, March and May 2014.

[22] Conversation with former French Ministry of Defense official No. 2, April 2014.

tions of power when they return to their home countries. In many cases, promotions tend to go to those officers who have established a relationship of trust with the leadership—not necessarily the most skilled or capable. This relational aspect is key and particularly important in small armies, which are common in Africa. Also, the partner nation's leadership may be reluctant to let go of someone they trust for several weeks or months, since that person may be difficult to replace with someone who is equally trusted or reliable. Countries that provide PME can at best be aware of these limitations, but have little say in the subsequent assignments and career of their alumni.[23]

Another challenge for France has been to build and maintain a relationship with students and alumni. Cuts in the defense budget have resulted in fewer resources being devoted to such activities as social and cultural events. Unlike in the United States, where social activities are generally included in PME packages to acclimate foreign students to the U.S. culture and way of life, budgets for such activities have declined dramatically in France. This represents a missed opportunity to further cement the relationship between promising foreign officers and the country to which they came to study.[24] Follow-up with alumni is also not as developed as it could be. For instance, the IHEDN alumni association has a very small budget, few activities, and is managed by rotating interns. One interviewee contrasted this situation with DoD's ACSS, which has an office in charge of alumni relations.[25]

Prospects for PME

Budgetary constraints may also affect the ENVR management structure. The Peacekeeping School of Bamako changed its status from an ENVR to an "International School." The key difference is in the number of countries that contribute financially to the management of the school. An ENVR is established by France and one partner nation; an international school has no limit on the number of donor countries

---

[23] Conversations with former French Ministry of Defense official No. 1, March and May 2014.

[24] Conversation with former French Ministry of Defense official No. 2, April 2014.

[25] Conversation with former French Ministry of Defense official No. 2, April 2014.

that can be part of the board of trustees that manages the school. In the Bamako school, France only has one *coopérant* left (as Director of Studies) and its financial contribution has fallen to €150,000 per year. Other contributors to the school are the United States, Canada, Germany, Japan, the Netherlands, and Switzerland.[26] More ENVRs may switch to the international school model in the future, especially as budgetary constraints become more and more severe. The challenge, however, is to find international partners willing to contribute financially to the enterprise.[27]

The next ENVR may be an international school, too. France has been looking to create a maritime security–focused ENVR at the strategic, rather than operational, level. A maritime security ENVR already exists in Equatorial Guinea but its target is low-level officers (captains, lieutenants) and enlisted personnel, and activities focus on crew training. The new school would also place particular emphasis on interagency and civil-military coordination, covering customs and merchant navy issues in addition to military ones. As of mid-2014, this project was still searching for international public and private funding.[28]

Advisory work

France regularly sends advisors to work closely with high-level officials—including chiefs of staff, defense ministers, or even presidents—for what is generally a three-year term. In 2014, the presidents of Côte d'Ivoire and the Central African Republic each had a French advisor.[29] France also has advisors in most regional organizations in Africa, including the AU, ECOWAS, the Economic Community of Central African

---

[26] "Les ENVR, une contribution à la paix . . . ," 2012, p. 29.

[27] Phone conversation with French Ministry of Foreign Affairs and International Development officials No. 2 and No. 3, August 2014.

[28] Phone conversation with French Ministry of Foreign Affairs and International Development officials No. 2 and No. 3, August 2014.

[29] Phone conversation with French Ministry of Foreign Affairs and International Development official No. 1, July 2014.

States, and the East African Community.[30] Advisors are *coopérants* who are integrated in the institutions of the partner nation. For instance, military advisors wear the uniform of the partner nation and report to two entities: their superior in the partner nation's army and the French DATT.[31] Advisors provide technical advice on how to organize defense institutions, including improving deployment capability, planning, and command (through map exercises, for instance); staffing and recruitment methods; logistics; or the budgetary system.[32]

France's role in advising partner nations in Africa has changed drastically over time. In the years that followed decolonization, "advisory" work was more akin to substitution—i.e., placing French officers where there should have been partner nations' officers—than support. Some French officers were even put in charge of African units.[33] Since the 1990s, France has shifted toward giving partner nations more ownership of the process. Budget cuts made this change even more critical and reinforced the notion that French *coopérants* should not play too large a role in partner nations' institutions and instead focus their action on high-level advice.

The role of French advisors in regional organizations varies between similar to a liaison and providing actual advice. France tends to be more present in organizations that are predominantly francophone, such as the Economic Community of Central African States, which hosted three French *coopérants* as of mid-2014.[34] Having a presence at the regional level is not only strategic, it also comes at a lesser

---

[30] Phone conversation with French Ministry of Foreign Affairs and International Development officials No. 2 and No. 3, August 2014.

[31] Conversations with former French Ministry of Defense official No. 1, March and May 2014.

[32] Phone conversation with French Ministry of Foreign Affairs and International Development official No. 1, July 2014.

[33] Phone conversation with French Ministry of Defense official No. 1, March 2014; phone conversation with Foreign Affairs and International Development officials No. 2 and No. 3, August 2014.

[34] Phone conversation with French Ministry of Foreign Affairs and International Development officials No. 2 and No. 3, August 2014.

cost than establishing a presence in all the countries belonging to that organization.[35]

The DCSD selects advisors based on several criteria. One is the individual's service of origin. Most francophone African countries have several French advisors who cover (when relevant) the army, navy, air force, the joint staff, the gendarmerie, ministries, or other key security agencies, and these advisors come from the same service or entity that they will be advising in the partner nation. Another criterion is ensuring a good fit between the skills of the advisor and those that will be most useful for the partner nation. A third criterion is the extent of the advisor's experience in Africa. A fourth important consideration is the rank of the advisor: countries that need a comprehensive action plan— for instance, in post-conflict situations—may welcome senior officers who will suggest important institutional changes. In other countries, where functional processes are already in place, the political and military leadership may be wary of potential encroachments of the former colonial power on their sovereignty and prefer less-senior officers. This is a delicate balance, however, since officers who are too junior may have insufficient legitimacy, in the eye of the partner nation, to discuss institutional reform with them. The DATT coordinates all the French advisors present in country.[36]

Besides individual advisors, France also sends small teams that perform audits of partner nation institutions. The DCSD reaches out to the relevant services (e.g., army, navy, police, gendarmerie) to identify candidates for the job.[37] Teams are built according to the needs and placed under the supervision of the DATT.[38] Their mandate can be shorter (a few days) or longer (a few months) depending on the requirements expressed by the partner nation. As an example, France did two

---

[35] Conversation with former French Ministry of Defense official No. 2, April 2014.

[36] Conversations with former French Ministry of Defense official No. 1, March and May 2014.

[37] Phone conversation with French Ministry of Foreign Affairs and International Development officials No. 2 and No. 3, August 2014.

[38] Conversations with former French Ministry of Defense official No. 1, March and May 2014.

such audits on Senegal's defense budget and its human resources.[39] Audits highlight gaps and offer recommendations, but do not systematically include an implementation plan. One interviewee described this as a chance for the partner country to take ownership of the institution building process by devising its own solutions to the problems highlighted by the audit team.[40]

Country Prioritization Process and Assessment of Requirements

The Ministry of Foreign Affairs and the Defense Minister jointly define priorities in Africa. These priorities are set in different forums. One is the annual meeting, where the National Defense General Secretariat (*Secrétariat général à la défense nationale*), which depends on the prime minister's office and the Ministry of Foreign Affairs, reviews all ongoing operations and African countries and determines France's strategic objectives in each. Other key institutional actors such the Joint Staff take part in this meeting.[41]

Another forum is the annual meetings of the Strategic Anticipation Groups (*groupes d'anticipation stratégique*) that include the Ministry of Foreign Affairs, intelligence services, the Joint Staff, and others to discuss key strategic directions for the coming years. These strategic directions are incorporated into guidance documents that get distributed to the different organizations involved and serve as a basis for action.[42]

Institutional actors involved in DIB get further guidance through the weekly meeting that takes place between the presidency's Africa advisor and the key officials involved in African security at the Ministry of Foreign Affairs, the Joint Staff, and intelligence services. Participants examine the countries that are particularly problematic and

---

[39] Phone conversation with French Ministry of Foreign Affairs and International Development officials No. 2 and No. 3, August 2014.

[40] Conversations with former French Ministry of Defense official No. 1, March and May 2014.

[41] Phone conversation with French Ministry of Defense official No. 1, March 2014.

[42] Phone conversation with French Ministry of Defense official No. 1, March 2014.

discuss solutions. The result of these brainstorming sessions may be papers for the presidency or for other institutions.[43]

France's strategic priorities are only half of the story. The other half is the request—or, at the very least, the willingness—of the partner nation. This is seen as an essential condition for the partner nation to be committed to cooperation projects. Partner nation commitment has become a key criterion in deciding where to conduct cooperation activities.[44] Some countries request lots of programs, while others do not. In some cases, requests follow an internal event. For instance, a new president may request an external audit of a security sector that was highly politicized during his predecessor's term.[45]

The DCSD is tasked with articulating cooperation plans for France's partner nations. These strategic plans first outline what France sees as important for the partner nation (e.g., safe borders, peacekeeping capability). This vision and related objectives get translated in guidance to ambassadors, joint commanders, defense attachés, and other relevant actors. It then gets operationalized through cooperation projects. Each of these three steps is validated by the partner nation. The French ambassador and the partner nation's chief of defense sign a convention by which they identify the actions to be taken and the schedule for their completion.[46]

Assessments

All cooperation projects get discussed and assessed during an annual meeting that includes all key institutional players. During the rest of

---

[43] Conversations with former French Ministry of Defense official No. 1, March and May 2014.

[44] Phone conversation with French Ministry of Foreign Affairs and International Development officials No. 2 and No. 3, August 2014.

[45] Conversations with former French Ministry of Defense official No. 1, March and May 2014.

[46] Conversations with former French Ministry of Defense official No. 1, March and May 2014.

the year, a permanent dialogue takes place between the DATT and Paris.[47]

France has made important changes in the process through which it used to assess its cooperation programs. The collapse of the Malian army in 2012, after many years of cooperation efforts on the part of France, as well as the difficulties that the AU and ECOWAS experienced in quickly deploying a peacekeeping force, may have weighed on the decision to make that change.[48]

Until recently, cooperation projects tended to be renewed on demand, even when they had little to show for the money spent. Now a greater emphasis falls on ensuring that the partner nation can, after three years (the usual timeline for DIB projects), have ownership of that project and sustain it without external assistance. One official interviewed cited as an example of a successful project the opening by France of a military center that provides job training for at-risk youth in Tunisia. Tunisia's involvement in the project was so successful that France decided its own value added was minimal, and pulled out after discussion with Tunis. Although this cooperation project is over for France, this experience encouraged funding more projects in Tunisia.[49]

The DCSD has also developed new methods to evaluate whether a project's objectives are being met, after realizing that it did not really have clear milestones against which to measure project progress.[50] France and the partner nation sign a convention that clearly states the project's duration, overall objective, and intermediary objectives. Each intermediary objective includes a list of actions to complete, and each

---

[47] Conversations with former French Ministry of Defense official No. 1, March and May 2014.

[48] Phone conversation with French Ministry of Foreign Affairs and International Development official No. 1, July 2014.

[49] Phone conversation with French Ministry of Foreign Affairs and International Development official No. 1, July 2014.

[50] Phone conversation with French Ministry of Foreign Affairs and International Development officials No. 2 and No. 3, August 2014.

action includes a description and a deadline.[51] Finally, the convention precisely describes each party's obligations and provides a detailed schedule.[52] Every six months, a Steering Committee gathers project managers to examine what actions have been completed—or not. These meetings also define priorities for the following six months. This new monitoring process was tested in 2012 and officially began in 2013 for new cooperation projects only.[53] This approach underlines that security cooperation is not just about building a relationship and establishing presence, but is rather a strategic tool to reach specific objectives, such as reinforcing African capacities. If the expected efforts by the partner nation fail to materialize, the DCSD director can issue several warnings to the partner nation and ultimately drop a cooperation project entirely.[54]

Another process that experienced recent change is the method through which requests for cooperation from partner nations are channeled to the DCSD. Instead of simply being on the receiving end of requests from DATTs, the DCSD now provides broad strategic considerations to guide the choice of cooperation projects. This new process is due to start in 2015 and went through a test phase in 2014. In January 2014, an internal working group within the DCSD delineated France's broad strategic priorities. The group submitted its list to the representatives of the regional bureaus within the Ministry of Foreign Affairs for review. The Joint Staff then validated it. Based on these priorities, DATTs sent back their requests by August 2014. The purpose of this reform is to make sure that every cooperation project has a purpose

---

[51] Phone conversation with French Ministry of Foreign Affairs and International Development officials No. 2 and No. 3, August 2014.

[52] Phone conversation with French Ministry of Foreign Affairs and International Development official No. 1, July 2014.

[53] Phone conversation with French Ministry of Foreign Affairs and International Development officials No. 2 and No. 3, August 2014.

[54] Phone conversation with French Ministry of Foreign Affairs and International Development official No. 1, July 2014.

that fits France's broader strategic priorities. France can also focus its action on its priority themes instead of having fragmented activities.[55]

France's Cooperation with Other DIB Providers

France frequently cooperates with other DIB providers in Africa, acknowledging that other actors may have a comparative advantage to undertake some types of activities or engage with particular countries. The European Union, for instance, has built expertise in SSR and its cooperation budget is larger than France's, making it better suited for a number of longer-term, comprehensive SSR efforts. The European Union also has an ability to promote norms in countries where similar efforts by France may be seen as neocolonialism. In a domain as sensitive, in terms of sovereignty, as DIB, European Union involvement is sometimes perceived as more politically acceptable than France's.[56]

Bilateral and multilateral cooperation often takes place at the DATT level. Attachés from different countries occasionally meet to discuss their ongoing activities. In practice, such information exchange takes place mostly at the bilateral level and according to personal affinities and personalities.[57]

Some programs present clear opportunities for cooperation. This is the case of the U.S. ACOTA program, which aims to increase the capacity of African countries to take part in peacekeeping operations, and the French program RECAMP (later EURORECAMP), whose purpose is to build the capacity of African countries. The two programs have activities that are largely complementary and, as a result, local implementers have made efforts to coordinate their action.[58] French Africa-based forces, as well as the DCSD in Paris, are in contact with ACOTA. This cooperation, however, is not institutionalized, possibly because the organizations and structures in charge of cooperation on each side of the Atlantic are different enough to make it difficult for

---

[55] Phone conversation with French Ministry of Foreign Affairs and International Development official No. 1, July 2014.

[56] Phone conversation with French Ministry of Defense official No. 1, March 2014.

[57] Conversation with former French Ministry of Defense official No. 2, April 2014.

[58] Phone conversation with French security cooperation official, July 2014.

each institution to find its equivalent and establish a formal dialogue.[59] A similar issue exists between France and the European Union. The latter focuses mostly on operational—rather than institutional—cooperation and, as result, the DCSD has no equivalent at the EU level.[60]

Conclusion: Insights from the French Experience and Recommendations for DoD

Through decades of doing DIB in Africa, France has accumulated a considerable number of lessons learned that can usefully inform its partner's own DIB activities in Africa. These include the following:

- Adapt the type and level of DIB effort to the partner nation. Post-conflict countries are more likely to accept major reforms, while countries sensitive to sovereignty issues will require a "lighter" set of recommendations.
- Obtain partner nation validation at every stage.
- Developing a good understanding of the institutional structure and political dynamics of the partner nation is key. It is particularly important to identify what institutions and individuals are central to the defense process. Key institutions and key individuals do not necessarily overlap and, in some instances, the path to enduring reform may lie as much through personal relationships as through institutions.
- Monitor projects closely to ensure they do not stall, either because of lack of will on the part of the partner nation or excessive red tape. Such monitoring is best done through on-site presence (as one interviewee put it, "remote reform does not work").[61]
- Remember that for DIB, multiyear time horizons are important. France sends advisors for what would be perceived in the United

[59] Phone conversation with French Ministry of Foreign Affairs and International Development officials No. 2 and No. 3, August 2014.

[60] Phone conversation with French Ministry of Foreign Affairs and International Development official No. 1, July 2014.

[61] Conversations with former French Ministry of Defense official No. 1, March and May 2014.

States as long periods (three years). It takes time for advisors to build relationships and understand all the political and institutional dynamics at play. In some countries, it is also more effective to export best practices over time rather than to push for large-scale, drastic reforms.

- Work with other DIB providers. Some partners of France have developed a "niche capability" in certain countries. France also relies increasingly on the European Union, which has serious SSR expertise, can sometimes more easily promote good governance norms than France, and has larger budgets to undertake long-term, comprehensive reform projects.

In addition to integrating some of these insights into its current DIB programs in Africa, another opportunity for DoD would be to become more involved in the ENVRs that already exist—as it has already done with the Peacekeeping School in Bamako—or to play a role in extending this concept to new countries and new educational focuses. These schools are relevant for DoD because the French are looking for multilateral partnerships with other Western countries and/or international organizations to help them fund these schools (and, presumably, the trainees who come from the region to these schools). For DoD, this means that they could benefit from structures that already exist. These schools also have the kind of regional dimension that would appeal to the United States.

Lessons from U.S. Allies: United Kingdom

Overview

UK DIB activities in North and West Africa are much smaller than those of the United States and France. They have focused mainly, although not exclusively, on Sierra Leone (site of the UK's largest—and most successful—example of DIB in recent years), Nigeria, and Ghana. UK DIB and other defense engagement work stresses UK cross-governmental cooperation. Assessment of DIB work emphasizes the overall national and regional effectiveness of DIB, rather than the success of individual programs or projects. The UK Parliament has stated concerns that the UK's limited resources in the area mean it is too ambitious in its hopes for affecting change in North and West Africa. It has called for closer work with the United States and France.

UK Understanding of DIB

The UK does not have a specific program dedicated to developing the high-level military and political institutions of other states. Instead, UK activities in this area form part of "defence diplomacy," which is a sub-section of the wider activities summarized in the 2013 International Defence Engagement Strategy (IDES).[62] While the UK has a long tradition of using its armed forces to train and develop the forces and defense institutions of other states, it is only since 1998 that it has distinguished such work as a separate policy area with dedicated funding.

The 2010 UK National Security Strategy and the Strategic Defence and Security Review that immediately followed it provided a renewed commitment by the UK government to work on defense engagement more broadly.[63] One outgrowth was the 2011 Building Stability Overseas Strategy, which provided a broad overview of what can drive instability and the steps that can be taken to address it.[64] The 2013 IDES then emerged as a response to the need identified in these documents for the UK's military to show greater commitment to upstream conflict prevention. It drew on the experiences and lessons of Afghanistan and Iraq and the work of the interagency-funded Conflict Prevention Pools. The IDES sets out how all defense activity short of combat operations is to be prioritized and focuses engagement efforts on "those countries which are most important to our national interests,

---

[62] Ministry of Defence (UK), *International Defence Engagement Strategy*, London, 2013.

[63] Ministry of Defence (UK), Cabinet Office, *A Strong Britain in an Age of Uncertainty: The National Security Strategy*, London: HMSO, 2010; Ministry of Defence (UK), *The Strategic Defence and Security Review*, London: HMSO, 2010.

[64] Department for International Development, Foreign and Commonwealth Office, and Ministry of Defence, *Building Stability Overseas Strategy*, London, 2011.

and where we are most likely to achieve the desired effect."[65] It operates with a planning time frame of 20 years and sets out four broad areas of activity:

1. *Security and "non-combat" operations*—including conventional deterrence and reassurance, embargoes and interdictions, security operations (e.g., maritime security, counterterrorism capability building), special forces, information operations, cyber security, and planning for non-combatant evacuation operations.

2. *Defence diplomacy*—direct engagement, including through senior-level visits; the DATT network; treaties and international arrangements; alliances and partnerships; civilian defense advisors; overseas and UK-based training and capacity building; work with multilateral organizations, including NATO, the EU, and the UN; loan service personnel; exchange and liaison officers and intelligence personnel working overseas; ship, unit, and aircraft visits.

3. *Defence and security exports*—support to British industry alongside UK Trade and Investment and Foreign and Commonwealth Office for the export of defense and security training, advice and material manufactured in the UK or by UK companies, in support of UK security objectives.

4. *Regional stability, conflict prevention, post-conflict reconstruction and stabilization*—including counter-proliferation, arms control, peacekeeping, SSR, stabilization, conflict prevention and reduction; frequently funded by the Conflict Pool in support of the Building Stability Overseas Strategy.

DIB activities come largely under defence diplomacy, but some DIB work may also be undertaken through activities that deal with regional stability, conflict prevention, and post-conflict reconstruction and stabilization.

---

[65] Ministry of Defence (UK), 2013, p. 3.

In undertaking international defense engagement work, the UK government has placed an increasing emphasis on cross-government work between the MoD, the Foreign and Commonwealth Office, DfID, the Stabilisation Unit, and other departments as required. DfID has perhaps the greatest room for maneuver in funding and experience at building overall state capacity. The MoD's international defense engagement work must therefore be seen as part of wider UK efforts. Because of their smaller size—at least in comparison to the United States'—UK activities tend to have more coherence and elicit interagency cooperation. Yet the system still suffers from departmental rivalry and an excess of strategic documents. The IDES is overseen by a senior-level Defence Engagement Board—jointly chaired by MoD and Foreign and Commonwealth Office officials—that provides strategic oversight of priorities both geographically and thematically and decides, in broad terms, how available resources should be allocated and what capabilities are required. Within the MoD, a Defence Strategy Group focuses on MoD efforts. The Defence Engagement Board takes into account a range of strategies including the Building Stability Overseas Strategy, CON-TEST (the UK's counterterrorism strategy), and specific strategies on issues ranging from countries at risk of instability and emerging powers to organized crime and counter proliferation.

Cooperation with allies tends to be ad hoc and country-specific. The three main partners for overall IDES work are the United States, France, and the EU. Cooperation with the United States is not as advanced as some officials or the UK Parliament would like.[66] British efforts at working with the United States are hindered by a perception that the scale of U.S. efforts leads them to be uncoordinated.[67] There are also language problems with France, largely when discussing defi-

---

[66] Interview with MoD official, May 2014; Foreign Affairs Committee, *The UK's response to extremism and instability in North and West Africa*, Seventh Report of Session 2013-14, HC86-I, March 21, 2014, pp. 48–50.

[67] Claire Spencer, *The UK's Response to Extremism and Political Instability in North and West Africa*, London: Chatham House, Parliamentary Evidence, May 2013.

nitions and concepts in advance of operations or when discussing long-term plans for the area.[68]

For the MoD, the IDES—and therefore DIB—has had a dual aim of upholding the reputation of the British military by flying the flag around the world, while also maintaining that military's relevance by providing it with activities that bring it into contact with a variety of security needs and non-Western militaries.[69] The British army has made a particular effort at international defense engagement, reflecting a desire to undertake new overseas activities to compensate for the end of large-scale operations such as in Afghanistan and Northern Ireland, as well as the British army's withdrawal from its bases in Germany. In the words of the current head of the British army, Sir Peter Wall, there is a need to maintain an "expeditionary mindset" to prevent the army from losing key skills that may be needed for future conflicts.[70]

Funding for IDES work can come from a variety of sources. In 2011, RAND estimated that total UK MoD spending on IDES was about $240 million, roughly 0.5 percent of the UK's defense budget. This included discretionary funds, the capitation costs of MoD officials, and attaché training.[71] Funding can also come from the Conflict Prevention Pools, a funding mechanism shared by the MoD, the Foreign and Commonwealth Office, and DfID that is designed to balance security and foreign policy needs with those of humanitarian and international development. In 2015, the pools are to be replaced by a "Conflict, Stability and Security Fund" totaling around $1.5 billion, with funding directed by the UK's National Security Council and accessible to all departments of UK government.

UK DIB Activities in North and West Africa
UK military activities in Africa are smaller than those of the United States and France. Britain tends to focus on countries that were part

---

[68] Interview with MoD official, May 2014.

[69] See Peter Wall and Allan Mallinson, *Defence Engagement: The British Army's Role in Building Security and Stability Overseas*, London: Chatham House, transcript, March 12, 2014.

[70] Wall and Mallinson, 2014.

[71] See Moroney, Gventer, et al., 2011.

of the British Empire. The UK has defense sections in its embassies in Algeria, Egypt, Ethiopia, Ghana, Libya, Morocco, Nigeria, Sierra Leone, and Somalia.[72] Through nonresident accreditation, they also cover Djibouti, Guinea, Côte d'Ivoire, Mali, Senegal, Gambia, Togo, and Tunisia.[73] In September 2012, the UK appointed a Sahel Special Envoy, the Rt. Hon. Stephen O'Brien MP. His job was initially focused on Mali and complemented a Sahel Taskforce headed by a former British ambassador to Morocco and Mauritania.[74] The UK has adopted a government-wide North and West Africa Strategic Approach, which it claims has led to a better understanding of the linkages, trends, and flows that extend across the region, including in the Sahel-Sahara region.[75] In 2014, the Foreign Office's Africa Directorate created a team of roaming officers to assist in London and across the Africa network, where necessary, and that could provide a surge capacity in the Sahel region if required.[76] The UK government has also indicated that, as a result of the drawdown from Afghanistan, Africa could become a focus of UK military efforts, both in international defense engagement and in more traditional operations and deployments. But the UK government is clear this will depend on funding and no clear plans are yet in place.[77]

As of early 2015, specific UK DIB work in North and West Africa was therefore quite limited and focused mostly on three countries: Ghana, Nigeria, and Sierra Leone.

From independence in 1957 through to 2009, Ghana was home to a range of British military training operations, with the British Military Advisory and Training Team (West Africa) assisting the Ghana-

---

[72] The UK embassy to Somalia is in Kenya.

[73] Andrew Murrison, parliamentary answer, House of Commons debate, December 17, 2013, col. 552W.

[74] Foreign Affairs Committee, 2014, p. 46.

[75] Foreign and Commonwealth Office, *Government's Response to the House of Commons Foreign Affairs Committee's Seventh Report of the Session 2013-2014 (HC86-I): The UK's Response to Extremism and Instability in North and West Africa,* London, May 2014

[76] Foreign and Commonwealth Office, 2014.

[77] Foreign and Commonwealth Office, 2014.

ian command and staff college from 1976–2009. It provided training advice and assistance to the management of the college. This included lectures, writing staff and technical exercises, and facilitating visiting lectures for the delivery of specialist defense modules. Starting in 2004, the team also assisted in the establishment of the Kofi Annan International Peacekeeping Training Center, with the team holding positions that included executive director, resource director and staff officer for training development. The team was funded through the tri-departmental Africa Conflict Prevention Program. The UK withdrew in 2009 as a result of MoD spending cuts.[78]

In Nigeria, the UK has long played a part in training the Nigerian military. In DIB-related work it has played a part in running the country's Defense College as part of wider efforts to improve leadership and doctrinal training, with a strong emphasis on ethics, behavior, the rule of law, human rights, strategic communications, logistics training, and maritime security cooperation.[79] The UK's efforts have often faced difficulties when the Nigerian government has been overthrown or faced periods of instability. Questions have increasingly been raised about both the Nigerian military's approach to human rights and the UK's ability to effect changes in training and ethics.[80] However, in 2014 the UK government stated it planed to strengthen its support in response to ongoing terrorist activity in the country.[81] Britain maintains a senior British military advisor to the Nigerian MoD and has developed capacity building programs through the office of Nigeria's national security adviser.[82] The UK has also contributed to EU funding and work in Nigeria to develop the Sahel Security College.[83] In a separate effort, DfID and the Foreign and Commonwealth Office have undertaken a

---

[78] See David Miliband, parliamentary answer, House of Commons debate, May 7, 2009, col. 361W.

[79] Foreign and Commonwealth Office, 2014.

[80] Interview with MOD official, May 2014.

[81] "Boko Haram Crisis: UK Boosts Nigeria Military Aid," *BBC News*, June 12, 2014.

[82] Foreign Affairs Committee, 2014, Ev 84.

[83] Foreign and Commonwealth Office, 2014.

range of activities to strengthen good governance and the resilience of the Nigerian state.[84]

The single largest and most successful recent example of UK DIB work in the region, however, remains Sierra Leone.[85] A former British colony, Sierra Leone started out in 1961 as one of the most stable states in West Africa. Several decades of poor governance and authoritarian rule and a devastating civil war lasting from 1991–2002 brought the country to an acute state of crisis. The UN peacekeeping mission (United Nations Mission in Sierra Leone, UNAMSIL) established in 1999 failed to bring the conflict under control, with the UN force itself coming close to collapse as its soldiers added to the prevailing lawlessness and instability. Operation PALLISER, an intervention by British forces in May 2000—initially intended to evacuate British and allied nationals—brought a halt to the fighting, allowed the UN mission to reorganize and reassert itself, and provided the opportunity for the democratic government to reassert control. In agreement with the democratic government, the UK signed a ten-year memorandum to lead international efforts to rebuild the Sierra Leonean state. Priorities and tasks were not set unilaterally by the UK but in full cooperation with the Sierra Leonean government, with the latter taking the lead. Between 2000 and 2013, the UK sponsored and delivered a wide range of nation-wide projects that had been agreed with the Sierra Leonean government. The British military was asked to lead the International Military Advisory and Training Team (IMATT), whose task was to completely rebuild Sierra Leone's MoD and armed forces.[86]

The UK's efforts encompassed a wide range of SSR activities. With the 17,500-strong UN force providing overall security, UK efforts were

---

[84] Foreign and Commonwealth Office, 2014.

[85] For overviews of the work undertaken in Sierra Leone, see Ashlee Godwin and Cathy Haenlein, "Security-Sector Reform in Sierra Leone: The UK Assistance Mission in Transition," *RUSI Journal*, Vol. 158, No. 6, 2013, pp. 30–39; and Harold Simpson, *UK Sponsored Stabilisation and Reform in Sierra Leone 2002–2013: A Unique Case or a Template for Future Intervention(s)?* Royal Military Academy Sandhurst, Sandhurst Occasional Papers, No. 19, 2014.

[86] This was not the first time the British military had worked in Sierra Leone, the UK having run a number of training missions before 1997.

able to focus on rebuilding basic military capabilities and developing new defense institutions as a part of wider efforts to promote national reconciliation. A decision was taken not to disband the remaining armed forces, but to rebuild them and integrate some former combatants from rebel groups. At a higher level, there was a need to start afresh with a new ministry of defense. Lt Col Harold Simpson, who was deployed to Sierra Leone as a member of IMATT, summarized UK efforts at DIB and the role this work played in wider efforts to rebuild the Sierra Leonean state:

> Advisors were embedded at both battalion and brigade level throughout the RSLAF's [Republic of Sierra Leone Armed Force's] 3 internally deployed brigades, the Air Wing, Maritime Wing and the operational headquarters known as the Joint Forces Command. At the governmental level the IMATT Commander (a British Army brigadier) was appointed as advisor to the Government of Sierra Leone on all security related matters with direct access to the President. Other IMATT military and senior UK civil servants were appointed to both executive and advisory roles within the Ministry of Defence to maintain the momentum of reform, reinforce the principle of civilian control of the military and guard against any return to the bad old days of military plotting and coups d'état. IMATT's activities were wide ranging and impacted at every level of the RSLAF, from overseeing recruiting and initial training up to strategic policy making and advising the Chief of Defence Staff, Deputy Defence Minister and President. It should also be pointed out that from the start IMATT worked closely with the DfID and the [Foreign and Commonwealth Office] funded Sierra Leone Security Sector Reform Programme, which further enshrined civilian control of the Armed Forces and transformed the architecture of the whole Security Sector with the establishment of the potentially neutral Office of National Security and Central Intelligence and Security Unit.[87]

DIB-related work was not assessed separately but as part of three wider national goals. First, that Sierra Leone would hold peaceful and

---

[87] Simpson, 2014.

effective democratic elections in which the military's role would be limited to providing security. Two such elections were held in 2007 and 2012. Second, that Sierra Leone would deploy a battalion as part of a UN peacekeeping mission. This goal was reached in 2009, when Sierra Leone was able to deploy a company to the UN mission in Darfur (2009–2013), followed by the deployment of a full battalion to the AU Mission in Somalia in June 2013. That UK military advisors were able to stand back and allow Sierra Leone to undertake the deployment to Somalia on their own was taken as the clearest signal that the UK had accomplished its mission. The third and final objective was to increase public support for the military, which was abysmally low in the immediate aftermath of the war. The results of British efforts proved extremely positive, with opinion polling showing that the Sierra Leonean military had gone from being one the most feared and corrupt national institutions to being its most respected and cherished, with only the nation's religious bodies considered less corrupt.[88] That UK efforts would in the future focus on the police—who in contrast were still seen as corrupt and threatening—was taken as a sign that reform of the military at all levels had worked. The UK scaled back its efforts in Sierra Leone in part due to the success of the mission and to Sierra Leone's move from post-conflict state to developing nation. Withdrawal was also the result of financial constraints and attention shifting to other states, such as Nigeria. IMATT was therefore transformed in 2013 into the much smaller International Security Assistance Team that now focuses on top-level change across the Sierra Leonean state, with special focus on the police and judiciary.

UK efforts in Sierra Leone provide several insights, some of which may be relevant for DIB work more generally. First, the UK benefitted from the fact that it was both seen as a legitimate player in Sierra Leone and had wide-ranging societal support in the country. Both the UK and Sierra Leone were keen to pursue a close relationship and, as such, the UK's role had a degree of legitimacy. This relationship was built on a positive history between the two countries, strong sustained support from key players such as UK Prime Minister Tony Blair and

---

[88] Transparency International, *Global Corruption Barometer 2013*, 2013, p. 37.

Sierra Leonean President Ahmed Kabbah, and wider support beyond the military, such as among civil servants and the country's middle class. Second, the UK was constantly careful to leave the front stage to the Sierra Leonean government. The close relationship between the two countries helped pave the way for and facilitate the delivery of the ten-year memorandum, which set limits, aims, and a long-term time-frame for the rebuilding of the country. Importantly, these aims were largely defined by Sierra Leone and not by the UK. Third, the UK had ample latitude to rebuild Sierra Leonean institutions. The end of the civil war provided a fresh start for the entire state, allowing the UK to reform in depth the Sierra Leonean MoD as part of a wider restart of state institutions. Fourth, UK efforts at DIB were part and parcel of wider efforts to reform other ministries. DIB formed part of the "comprehensive approach" driven by the Foreign and Commonwealth Office, DfID, and MoD triumvirate. Fifth, the mission was of a manageable size for the UK. The UK bore about 85–90 percent of the overall costs and, in the earlier phases—before the Iraq and Afghan wars drew away resources—was able to draw on its best soldiers and civil servants. There were also no external security challenges or threats to Sierra Leone, which might have necessitated wider and more direct UK military involvement.

Wider DIB Work in Africa

The MoD runs in-country courses across Africa and welcomes staff from African nations to the Royal College of Defence Studies in London. Examples include the range of in-country courses in Sudan and the Strategic Security Partnership with Algeria that has facilitated delivery of specialized UK-based courses for Algerian military officers.[89]

One of the best examples of UK DIB efforts in Africa came with the end of South Africa's apartheid regime. The UK led international assistance to create a new South African MoD. This entailed the presence of a one-star British officer for a couple of years in the South African MoD. As of 2015, the UK retains two officers at the South African War College and there remains a long-standing interest from South

---

[89] Lord Ahmad of Wimbledon, House of Lords debate, March 27, 2014, col. 585

Africa in sending people on UK courses such as the Royal College of Defence Studies.[90]

In Libya, a UK Defence Advisory and Training Team was established in Tripoli in 2012 with the intention of providing advice through a number of personnel embedded in the Libyan MoD. The team was withdrawn in August 2014 due to the deteriorating security situation. The team provided specialist advice on defense reform, disarmament, and border security and did so through a range of programs on strategic communication, developing explosive ordinance disposal schools, naval training, and the creation of a joint operational planning capability.[91] Some training was also undertaken in the UK on courses at institutions such as the Maritime Warfare School and the Joint Services Command and Staff College.[92]

Assessing DIB

The 2011 RAND report *Lessons from U.S. Allies in Security Cooperation with Third Countries* noted that the UK did not have any formal assessment and lessons-learned process to inform UK defense diplomacy.[93] Attachés, training teams (whether short or long term), visits (including ship visits and senior officer visits), and exercises produce or generate any number of reports. These inform the regional desk officers in the MoD's joint staff directorates, who are expected to pass on this information to the individual services. In turn, the individual service staffs are expected to assimilate this information and adjust their planning and descriptions of future intentions accordingly. In doing so, the UK has tended to use the term "lessons identified" rather than "lessons learned" to differentiate between reporting a lesson and acting on it.[94]

---

[90] Interview with MoD official, May 2014.

[91] Philip Dunne, parliamentary answer, House of Commons debate, November 11, 2014, col. W.

[92] Andrew Robathan, parliamentary answer, House of Commons debate, September 17, 2011, col. 458W.

[93] Moroney, Gventer, et al., 2011, p. 71.

[94] Moroney, Gventer, et al., 2011, p. 71.

The 2011 RAND report noted a recognition that the UK MoD's contributions to and use of defense diplomacy and other soft power tools was problematic because of a paucity of resources, difficulties delivering the objectives set down, and, in some instances, little connection between activities and what they were achieving. As the report noted, this does not mean the UK programs are ineffective, "more that this points to a perennial difficulty with soft power: measures of effectiveness."[95] This difficulty remains in place today. The Building Stability Overseas Strategy places great importance on being able to rigorously measure whether public confidence is growing in the ability of a fragile state to deliver the things the people in that state most care about, such as jobs, security, and justice. But as one interviewee highlighted with regard to measuring projects and their effectiveness: "The MoD accepts that this is a judgment and not an exact science. There is no answer to the problem of performance monitoring, and our most important aim is to measure influence."[96]

The clearest example of UK success in DIB activity is the aforementioned efforts in Sierra Leone. However, given the breadth of activities undertaken as part of the wider operation that DIB activities were a part of, it becomes difficult to isolate DIB performance against the wider success of the overall mission. DIB is also a long-term effort and, as a result, it remains to be seen whether concepts such as neutrality, loyalty to institutions, and civilian oversight have been truly assimilated and will stand the test of time.

In reviewing the IDES, the House of Commons Defence Committee made clear its concerns about how progress in this area is measured.[97] In reply, the MoD stated:

> When measuring the effectiveness of international defence engagement, it is usually impossible to link progress towards UK goals to specific activities (such as the attendance of an individ-

---

[95] Moroney, Gventer, et al., 2011, p. 67.

[96] Interview with MoD official, May 2014.

[97] House of Commons Defence Committee, *Intervention: Why, When and How?* Fourteenth Report of Session 2013–14, Vol. 1, HC 952, April 28, 2014a, p. 6.

ual on a UK defence training course). The MOD has therefore taken an outcomes-based approach, using a metric (the "Maturity Model") to measure overall progress against UK MOD objectives, including in securing access, basing and over flight rights; capacity building; building influence; supporting UK trade and exports; and defence industry cooperation. Like most of the benefits of defence engagement, the outcomes we measure are long term, and subject to buffeting by events, and so while we measure the maturity of our outcomes against our objectives now, the real importance of these metrics is the change we will see in the next 5 to 10 years.[98]

The Defence Committee also made clear it wanted to see progress in creating a "unified vocabulary" to be used across government and a willingness to share mistakes and lessons learned.[99] The committee also voiced a concern that Britain's international defense engagement has become detached from the general public's understanding of what the UK does when it is involved in military activities around the world. According to the committee, there is little public awareness of the range of overseas activities that the UK carries out, including DIB, and this failure has potential political and security costs thanks to the public's reluctance to support such operations.[100] Finally, UK efforts in North and West Africa—whether DIB, wider military work, or other UK-sponsored activities—has come under criticism for being too ambitious. In a 2013 inquiry into extremism in North and West Africa, the House of Commons Foreign Affairs Committee, while supportive of the UK government's desire to tackle extremism in the area, criticized the mismatch between ambitions and capabilities. The Foreign and Commonwealth Office, in particular, was castigated for tending toward the aspirational rather than the specific when outlining strategic approaches to the region, leaving the committee with no clear

---

[98] House of Commons Defence Committee, *Intervention: Why, When and How?: Government Response to the Committee's Fourteenth Report of Session 2013–14*, Fourth Special Report of Session 2014–15, HC 581, July 29, 2014b.

[99] House of Commons Defence Committee, 2014a, p. 8.

[100] House of Commons Defence Committee, 2014a, pp. 7 and 101.

sense of how the UK would prioritize and organize its work in the area or whom its main partners would be. The committee stated:

> The Prime Minister appears to have committed the UK to a more ambitious programme of bilateral engagement in North and West Africa, in addition to increased partnership working. In his January 2013 statement to the House, he committed the UK to "work right across the region" to help address "weak political institutions, political instability and a failure to address long-standing political grievances" and pledged that the UK would help put in place "the building blocks of democracy—the rule of law and the independence of the judiciary, the rights of minorities, free media and association, and a proper place in society for the army." In its submission to this inquiry, the [Foreign and Commonwealth Office] set out a similar vision, referring to a new approach to North and West Africa, based around three pillars of security, development and politics.

> These ambitions should be set against the UK's diplomatic footprint in the Western Sahel, which is very light. The Africa Minister, Mr. Simmonds, told us that the UK has some 1000 staff based in the region relevant to this report. We suggest that this statistic gives a somewhat misleading impression of the depth of the UK's current engagement: in the first place because it includes staff of all UK government departments and agencies and secondly because we understand the reference to include all the countries in West and North Africa, including countries such as Egypt and Ghana, where the UK has relatively large embassies. In relation to the countries of the Western Sahel, we consider it important to spell out just out low our current diplomatic representation is: the UK has one small embassy in Bamako, Mali, employing fewer than five UK-based staff, and no embassies in Chad, Niger, Burkina Faso or Mauritania. As we understand it, the total number of UK-based staff (of any department) currently working in all of these countries is well under ten.

> In the Maghrebi states of Morocco, Algeria and Libya, the UK's diplomatic profile is a little higher than in West Africa, although

none of the three embassies is large and all three, we understand, are dwarfed by those of France and the U.S.

In conclusion, the committee made clear that: "The Government should consider increasing its resources in the region and its reserves of specialist knowledge. If not, it should scale back its ambitions—and its rhetoric."[101]

Lessons for the United States

The UK's engagement in DIB activities offer five specific lessons that could be emulated by other DIB providers, including the United States.

Assessments should focus on local perceptions of institutions. UK assessments of DIB work have tended to focus on overall effectiveness rather than individual programs and acknowledge the inherent limits of this exercise, which incorporates a large amount of judgment. The single most important measurement is public confidence in the ability of the state to deliver those services the population most cares about, such as jobs, security, and justice. Focusing on UK or U.S.-defined goals risks alienating not only the partner government, but also its citizens.

Ambitions should match resources. The UK Parliament has been critical of the UK government being too ambitious in North and West Africa, urging it either to increase resources or scale back aspirations. Success in Sierra Leone was achieved, in part, because of its manageable size, strong political support in both the UK and Sierra Leone, resources being available, and a long-term time frame in which to deliver. The UK Parliament has also noted some ambiguity in the language used to describe interventions. The language often focuses on direct military intervention, when other less-prominent interventions such as DIB and IDES also need to be taken into account. This is important for public understanding and support.[102] Success is unlikely without a long-term political commitment to commit resources,

---

[101] Foreign Affairs Committee, 2014, p. 47.

[102] House of Commons Defence Committee, 2014a, pp. 45–46.

embrace pragmatism, and show patience for a process that can take a long time before it starts showing results.

DIB requires a whole-of-government approach. One of the strengths of UK efforts in Sierra Leone was that they involved more than the MoD and military and reached across various governmental agencies. There will always be tensions, not least between the military and international development spheres, but both sides need to overcome suspicions to recognize the importance of their combined work and ensure they can draw on the full-range of skills in both the military and from across government. This would also allow the military to develop the cultural skills necessary to work with the local populations and to appreciate the local specificities that will shape effective and legitimate defense institutions. With regard to assessments, the military could also seek to draw on the often better-developed, more holistic and, at times, better-funded assessment frameworks provided by departments such as DfID or aid agencies.

Greater DIB collaboration among the United States, United Kingdom, and France may be quite valuable. The UK has interests in North and West Africa but has limited resources with which to pursue its objectives. This means it is keen to work with others, especially the United States and France. If these three allies can coordinate effectively, they may be able to draw in other NATO contributors to expand DIB efforts across Africa.

Effective DIB work requires political and cultural awareness of the partner nation. The UK's MoD is also keen to improve working knowledge of regions such as North and West Africa, something it has begun to do through regionally aligned forces. This move is also recognition that UK efforts (whether on its own or with allies) in one country will be limited without an awareness of and ability to affect change in the wider region.

Abbreviations

ACOTA	Africa Contingency Operations Training and Assistance
ACSS	Africa Center for Security Studies
AFL	Armed Forces of Liberia
AFRICOM	U.S. Africa Command
AMEP	African Military Education Program
AU	African Union
CCP	country cooperation plan
DASD	deputy assistant secretary of defense
DATT	defense attaché
DCSD	*Direction de la Coopération de Sécurité et de Défense*
DEEP	Defense Education Enhancement Program
DfID	Department for International Development
DIB	defense institution building
DIILS	Defense Institute of International Legal Studies
DIRI	Defense Institutional Reform Initiative
DoD	U.S. Department of Defense
DRC	Democratic Republic of the Congo

DSCA	Defense Security Cooperation Agency
ECOWAS	Economic Community of West African States
ENVR	*écoles nationales à vocation régionale* (regionally oriented national school)
FMF	foreign military financing
FY	fiscal year
ICS	integrated country strategy
IDES	International Defence Engagement Strategy (UK)
IHEDN	*Institut de hautes études de defense nationale* (Institute for Higher National Defense Studies)
IIAG	Ibrahim Index of African Governance
IMATT	International Military Advisory and Training Team
IMET	International Military Education and Training
IMO	intermediate military objective
LOE	line of effort
MoD	Ministry of Defense
MoDA	Ministry of Defense Advisors Program
NATO	North Atlantic Treaty Organization
NESA	Near East and South Asia Center for Strategic Studies
NSC	National Security Council
OECD	Organization for Economic Co-operation and Development
OOL	Operation Onward Liberty
OSD	Office of the Secretary of Defense
PfP	Partnership for Peace

PME	professional military education
PPD	presidential policy directive
SDO	senior defense official
SGI	Security Governance Initiative
SPP	State Partnership Program
SSG	security sector governance
SSR	security sector reform
TCP	theater campaign plan
UCMJ	Uniform Code of Military Justice
UNDP	United Nations Development Programme
UNMIL	United Nations Mission in Liberia
UNSMIL	United Nations Support Mission in Libya
WIF	Wales (formerly Warsaw) Initiative Fund

Bibliography

Africa Center for Strategic Studies, *ACSS Program Schedule FY2014*, Washington, D.C., October 24, 2013. As of May 13, 2015:
http://africacenter.org/wp-content/uploads/2013/11/FY14-Program-Schedule-EN.pdf

Africa Center for Strategic Studies, *FY2014 Program Plan*, December 12, 2013.

African Union Commission, *African Union Policy Framework on Security Sector Reform*, Addis Ababa, Ethiopia, undated. As of October 14, 2015:
http://www.peaceau.org/uploads/au-policy-framework-on-security-sector-reform-ae-ssr.pdf

African Union Peace and Security, "The African Standby Force (ASF)," web page, updated April 19, 2015. As of May 1, 2015:
http://www.peaceau.org/en/page/82-african-standby-force-asf-amani-africa-1

Andrews, Matt, *The Limits of Institutional Reform in Development: Changing Rules for Realistic Solutions*, New York: Cambridge University Press, January 2014.

Ball, Nicole, "Reforming Security Sector Governance," *Conflict, Security & Development*, Vol. 4, No. 3, 2004, pp. 509–527.

Ball, Nicole, J. Kayode Fayemi, Funmi Olonisakin, Martin Rupiya, and Rocklyn Williams, "Governance in the Security Sector," in Nicolas van de Walle, Nicole Ball, and Vijaya Ramachandran (eds.), *Beyond Structural Adjustment: The Institutional Context of African Development*, New York: Palgrave Macmillan, 2003, pp. 263–304.

Ball, Nicole, and Michael Brzoska, with Kees Kingma and Herbert Wulf, "Voice and Accountability in the Security Sector," Bonn International Center for Conversion, Paper 21, July 2002.

Ben Barka, Habiba, and Mthuli Ncube, *Political Fragility in Africa: Are Military Coups d'Etat a Never-Ending Phenomenon?* African Development Bank, September 2012.

Benkert, Joseph A., "Policy Priorities for DoD Regional Centers Program Planning, 2010–2015," memorandum to the directors of DSCA and the regional centers, February 1, 2008.

Blanchard, Christopher M., *Libya: Transition and U.S. Policy*, Washington, D.C.: Congressional Research Service, RL33142, September 8, 2014.

———, *Libya: Transition and U.S. Policy*, Washington, D.C.: Congressional Research Service, RL33142, August 3, 2015.

Blaney, John, Jacques Paul Klein, and Sean McFate, *Wider Lessons for Peacebuilding: Security Sector Reform in Liberia*, Muscatine, Ia.: The Stanley Foundation, June 2010.

Boucher, Alix Julia, *Defense Sector Reform: A Note on Current Practice*, Henry L. Stimson Center, December 12, 2009.

"Boko Haram Crisis: UK Boosts Nigeria Military Aid," *BBC News*, June 12, 2014. As of May 15, 2015:
http://www.bbc.co.uk/news/world-africa-27812766

Bryden, Alan, and Fummi Olonisakin, eds., *Security Sector Transformation in Africa*, Munster: LIT Verlag, 2010.

Cook, Nicolas, *Liberia's Post-War Development: Key Issues and U.S. Assistance*, Washington, D.C.: Congressional Research Service, RL33185, May 19, 2010. As of October 14, 2015:
http://fas.org/sgp/crs/row/RL33185.pdf

Commander, U.S. Africa Command, *AFRICOM Theater Campaign, Plan 7000-10*, January 25, 2010.

———, *AFRICOM Theater Campaign, Plan 7000-12*, January 25, 2012.

———, *AFRICOM Theater Campaign Plan 2000-16, Fiscal Years 2016-2020*, August 2015. Not available to the general public.

d'Andurain, Jean, and Alan G. Stolberg, "Defense Education Enhancement Program: The NATO Functional Clearing-House on Defense Education," *Connections: The Quarterly Journal*, Vol. 11, No. 4, Fall 2012, pp. 53–58.

Defense Institute of International Legal Studies, *Annual Report Fiscal Year 2012*, Newport, R.I., 2013. As of September 22, 2014:
https://www.diils.org/resource/diils-report-fy12-13-aug2pdf

———, "In Congo (DRC) DILLS Conducts Its Largest Seminar," web page, March 12, 2014. As of July 2014:
https://www.diils.org/fr/news-story/congo-drc-diils-conducts-its-largest-seminar

Defense Institute of Security Assistance Management, *Security Cooperation Programs Through Fiscal Year 2014*, Revision 14.2, undated. As of July 2014:
http://www.disam.dsca.mil/documents/pubs/security_cooperation_programs_3Feb2014.pdf

Defense Institutional Reform Initiative, *Concept for Defense Institution Building (DIB) Assessment in Libya*, undated. Not available to the general public.

———, "Concept for DIRI Support to Liberian Ministry of Defense," June 7, 2012. Not available to the general public.

———, "Building Defense Institutional Capacity," briefing, September 2013.

Defense Security Cooperation Agency, *Regional Centers for Security Studies: FY2011 Annual Report*, undated.

———, *Fiscal Year 2012 Budget Estimates*, February 2011.

———, *Security Assistance Management Manual*, April 30, 2012. As of October 16, 2015:
http://www.samm.dsca.mil/listing/chapters

———, *Fiscal Year 2014 Budget Estimates*, April 2013.

———, *Fiscal Year 2015 Budget Estimates*, March 2014.

———, *Fiscal Year 2016 Budget Estimates*, February 2015. As of May 13, 2015:
http://comptroller.defense.gov/Portals/45/Documents/defbudget/fy2016/budget_
justification/pdfs/01_Operation_and_Maintenance/O_M_VOL_1_PART_1/
DSCA_PB16.pdf

Department for International Development, Foreign and Commonwealth Office, and Ministry of Defence, *Building Stability Overseas Strategy*, London, 2011.

DIILS—*See* Defense Institute of International Legal Studies.

DIRI—*See* Defense Institution Reform Initiative.

DSCA—*See* Defense Security Cooperation Agency.

Dulait, André, Robert Hue, Yves Pozzo di Borgo, and Didier Boulaud, "La France et la gestion des crises africaines: quels changements possibles?" French Senate, Committee on Foreign Affairs, Information Report No. 405 (2005–2006), July 3, 2006. As of October 16, 2015:
http://www.senat.fr/rap/r05-450/r05-450.html

Dunne, Philip, parliamentary answer, House of Commons debate, November 11, 2014, col. W. As of October 14, 2015:
http://www.parliament.uk/business/publications/
written-questions-answers-statements/written-question/
Commons/2014-11-04/213193/

Edelman, Eric S., "Policy Guidance for the DOD Regional Centers," memorandum, January 18, 2008.

European Union External Action, "EU Integrated Border Assistance Mission in Libya (EUBAM Libya)," fact sheet, January 2015. As of October 14, 2015:
http://www.eeas.europa.eu/csdp/missions-and-operations/eubam-libya/pdf/
factsheet_eubam_libya_en.pdf

Flournoy, Michèle, "Policy Guidance for the Department of Defense (DoD) Regional Centers," memorandum to regional center directors, February 28, 2011.

Foreign Affairs Committee, *The UK's response to extremism and instability in North and West Africa*, Seventh Report of Session 2013-14, HC86-I, March 21, 2014.

Foreign and Commonwealth Office, *Government's Response to the House of Commons Foreign Affairs Committee's Seventh Report of the Session 2013-2014 (HC86-I): The UK's Response to Extremism and Instability in North and West Africa*, London, May 2014.

French Ministry of Defense, *Livre Blanc Défense et sécurité nationale [White Paper on Defense and National Security]*, 2013.

Garrett, William B., III, "Forward in Africa: USAFRICOM and the U.S. Army in Africa," web page, U.S. Army Africa, January 10, 2010. As of October 14, 2015: http://www.usaraf.army.mil/NEWS/NEWS_100110_FORWARD_AFRICA.html

Geneva Center for the Democratic Control of Armed Forces, "Who We Are," web page, undated. As of June 2014: http://www.dcaf.ch/

Ginifer, Jeremy, "The Challenges of the Security Sector and Security Reform Processes in Democratic Transitions: The Case of Sierra Leone," *Democratization*, Vol. 13, No. 5, 2006.

Godwin, Ashlee, and Cathy Haenlein, "Security-Sector Reform in Sierra Leone: The UK Assistance Mission in Transition," *RUSI Journal*, Vol. 158, No. 6, 2013, pp. 30–39.

Gompert, David C., Olga Oliker, Brooke Stearns Lawson, Keith Crane, and K. Jack Reilly, *Making Liberia Safe: Transformation of the National Security Sector*, Santa Monica, Calif.: RAND Corproration, MG-529-OSD, 2007. As of October 14, 2015: http://www.rand.org/pubs/monographs/MG529.html

Ham, Carter, *USAFRICOM Posture Statement*, various years (2011, 2012, and 2013).

Hanauer, Larry, Stuart E. Johnson, Christopher J. Springer, Chaoling Feng, Michael J. McNerney, Stephanie Pezard, and Shira Efron, *Evaluating the Impact of the Department of Defense Regional Centers for Security Studies*, Santa Monica, Calif.: RAND Corporation, RR-388-OSD, 2014. As of October 27, 2015: http://www.rand.org/pubs/research_reports/RR388.html

Hänngi, Heiner, *The Challenges of Security Sector Governance*, Geneva Center for the Democratic Control of Armed Forces, 2003.

Hänngi, Heiner, and Fred Tanner, "Promoting Security Sector Governance in the EU's Neighbourhood," *Chaillot Paper*, No. 80, European Union Institute for Security Studies, July 2005.

Hooper, Charles W., "United States Africa Command: Theater Synchronization," briefing, AFRICOM Strategy, Plans, and Programs (J5), June 7, 2013.

House of Commons Defence Committee, *Intervention: Why, When and How?* Fourteenth Report of Session 2013–14, Vol. 1, HC 952, April 28, 2014a. As of October 15, 2015:
http://www.publications.parliament.uk/pa/cm201314/cmselect/cmdfence/952/952.pdf

———, *Intervention: Why, When and How?: Government Response to the Committee's Fourteenth Report of Session 2013–14*, Fourth Special Report of Session 2014–15, HC 581, July 29, 2014b. As of October 15, 2015:
http://www.publications.parliament.uk/pa/cm201415/cmselect/cmdfence/581/581.pdf

Howe, Herbert M., *Ambiguous Order: Military Forces in African States*, Lynne Rienner Publishers, 2001.

Inter-American Air Forces Academy, brochure, Lackland Air Force Base, Tex.: U.S. Air Force, undated. As of September 25, 2015:
http://www.37trw.af.mil/shared/media/document/AFD-121221-016.pdf

International Crisis Group, *Liberia: Uneven Progress in Security Sector Reform*, Crisis Group Africa Report No. 148, January 13, 2009.

Joint Chiefs of Staff, *Security Force Assistance*, Joint Doctrine Note 1-13, April 29, 2013.

Kapp, Lawrence, and Nina M. Serafino, *The National Guard State Partnership Program: Background, Issues, and Options for Congress*, Washington, D.C.: Congressional Research Service, R41957, August 15, 2011. As of October 15, 2015:
https://www.fas.org/sgp/crs/misc/R41957.pdf

"Les ENVR, une contribution à la paix, la stabilité et la sécurité en Afrique subsaharienne [ENVRs, a contribution to peace, stability and security in Sub-Saharan Africa]," *Partenaires Sécurité Défense*, No. 268, Winter 2012.

"Les ressources humaines [Human Resources]," *Partenaires Sécurité Défense*, Vol. 274, June 2014. As of October 16, 2015 :
http://www.diplomatie.gouv.fr/fr/IMG/pdf/PSD_274__web_3_cle8beec5-1.pdf

Liberia Executive Mansion, "At 57th Armed Forces Day Anniversary, Commander-in-Chief Sirleaf Commissions New Liberian Leadership; Urges Them to Lead by Example," press release, February 11, 2014. As of February 2015:
http://www.emansion.gov.lr/2press.php?news_id=2892&related=7&pg=sp

Liberia Executive Mansion, "Speech by H.E. Madam Ellen Johnson Sirleaf, President and Commander-in-Chief of the Armed Forces of Liberia on the 57th Armed Forces Day," Speeches, February 11, 2014. As of February 2015:
http://www.emansion.gov.lr/doc/President_2014_Armed_Forces_Day_Speech(FINAL).pdf

Lord Ahmad of Wimbledon, House of Lords debate, March 27, 2014, col. 585. As of October 16, 2015:
http://www.publications.parliament.uk/pa/ld201314/ldhansrd/text/140327-0001.htm

Lorgeoux, Jeanny, and Jean-Marie Bockel, "L'Afrique est notre avenir," French Senate, Committee on Foreign Affairs, Defence and Armed Forces, Information Report No. 104 (2013–2014), October 29, 2013. As of October 16, 2015:
http://www.senat.fr/rap/r13-104/r13-10465.html

Marks, Edward, "Why USAFRICOM?" *Joint Force Quarterly*, Vol. 52, January 2009.

McFate, Sean, *Building Better Armies: An Insider's Account of Liberia*, Carlisle Barracks, Penn.: U.S. Army War College, Strategic Studies Institute and Peacekeeping and Stabilization Operations Institute, 2013.

McNerney, Michael J., Angela O'Mahony, Thomas Szayna, Derek Eaton, Caroline Baxter, Colin P. Clarke, Emma Cutrufello, Michael McGee, Heather Peterson, Leslie Adrienne Payne, andCalin Trenkov-Wermuth, *Assessing Security Cooperation as a Preventive Tool*, Santa Monica, Calif.: RAND Corporation, RR-350-A, 2014. As of October 22, 2015:
http://www.rand.org/pubs/research_reports/RR350.html

McNerney, Michael J., Christopher M. Schnaubelt, Agnes Gereben Schaefer, Martina Melliand, and Bill Gelfeld, *Improving DoD Support to FEMA's All-Hazards Plans*, Santa Monica, Calif.: RAND Corporation, RR-1301-OSD, 2015. As of December 9, 2015:
http://www.rand.org/pubs/research_reports/RR1301.html

Miliband, David, parliamentary answer, House of Commons debate, May 7, 2009, col. 361W. As of October 15, 2015:
http://www.parliament.the-stationery-office.co.uk/pa/cm200809/cmhansrd/cm090507/text/90507w0008.htm

Ministry of Defence (UK), Cabinet Office, *A Strong Britain in an Age of Uncertainty: The National Security Strategy*, London: HMSO, 2010.

Ministry of Defence (UK), *The Strategic Defence and Security Review*, London: HMSO, 2010.

———, *International Defence Engagement Strategy*, London, 2013.

Ministry of National Defense (Liberia), *National Defense Strategy of the Republic of Liberia*, February 11, 2014.

Mo Ibrahim Foundation, "2014 IIAG Methodology," 2014. As of March 20, 2015:
http://www.moibrahimfoundation.org/downloads/publications/2014/2014-iiag-methodology.pdf

Moroney, Jennifer D. P., Beth Grill, Joe Hogler, Lianne Kennedy-Boudali, and Christopher Paul, *How Successful Are U.S. Efforts to Build Capacity in Developing Countries? A Framework to Assess the Global Train and Equip "1206" Program*, Santa Monica, Calif.: RAND Corporation, TR-1121-OSD, 2011. As of October 27, 2015:
http://www.rand.org/pubs/technical_reports/TR1121.html

Moroney, Jennifer D. P., Celeste Gventer, Stephanie Pezard, and Laurence Smallman, *Lessons from U.S. Allies in Security Cooperation with Third Countries: The Cases of Australia, France, and the United Kingdom*, Santa Monica, Calif.: RAND Corporation, TR-972-AF, 2011. As of October 15, 2015:
http://www.rand.org/pubs/technical_reports/TR972.html

Moroney, Jennifer D. P., Joe Hogler, Jefferson P. Marquis, Christopher Paul, John E. Peters, and Beth Grill, *Developing an Assessment Framework for U.S. Air Force Building Partnerships Programs*, Santa Monica, Calif.: RAND Corporation, MG-868-AF, 2010. As of October 27, 2015:
http://www.rand.org/pubs/monographs/MG868.html

Moroney, Jennifer D. P., Joe Hogler, Lianne Kennedy-Boudali, and Stephanie Pezard, *Integrating the Full Range of Security Cooperation Programs into Air Force, Planning: An Analytic Primer*, Santa Monica, Calif.: RAND Corporation, TR-974-AF, 2011. As of October 22, 2015:
http://www.rand.org/pubs/technical_reports/TR974.html

Moroney, Jennifer D. P., David E. Thaler, and Joe Hogler, *Review of Security Cooperation Mechanisms Combatant Commands Utilize to Build Partner Capacity*, Santa Monica, Calif.: RAND Corporation, RR-413-OSD, 2013. As of October 15, 2015:
http://www.rand.org/pubs/research_reports/RR413.html

Murrison, Andrew, parliamentary answer, House of Commons debate, December 17, 2013, col. 552W. As of October 16, 2015:
http://www.publications.parliament.uk/pa/cm201314/cmhansrd/cm131217/text/131217w0001.htm#131217w0001.htm_spnew57

National Guard, "State Partnership Program," web page, undated. As of January 2015:
http://www.nationalguard.mil/Leadership/JointStaff/J5/InternationalAffairsDivision/StatePartnershipProgram.aspx

National Guard, State Partnership Program map, July 1, 2015. As of October 16, 2015:
http://www.nationalguard.mil/Portals/31/Documents/J-5/InternationalAffairs/StatePartnershipProgram/SPP%20Map%20(Jul%2001%202015).pdf

NATO—*See* North Atlantic Treaty Organization.

Near East and South Asia Center for Strategic Studies, unpublished FY2013-2014 Program Plan, May 11, 2012.

North Atlantic Treaty Organization, "Istanbul Summit Communiqué," press release, June 28, 2004. As of September 17, 2015:
http://www.nato.int/docu/pr/2004/p04-096e.htm

OECD—*See* Organisation for Economic Co-operation and Development.

Office of the Inspector General, *Defense Institution Reform Initiative Program Elements Need to Be Defined*, Washington, D.C.: Department of Defense, DODIG-2013-019, November 9, 2012.

Organisation for Economic Co-operation and Development, *OECD DAC Handbook on Security System Reform: Supporting Security and Justice*, Paris: OECD Publishing, February 2007a. As of October 19, 2015:
http://www.oecd-ilibrary.org/development/
the-oecd-dac-handbook-on-security-system-reform_9789264027862-en

―――, "Principles for Good International Engagement in Fragile States and Situations," April 2007b. As of October 15, 2015:
http://www.oecd.org/dacfragilestates/43463433.pdf

Ouédraogo, Emile, *Advancing Military Professionalism in Africa*, Washington D.C.: Africa Center for Strategic Studies, Research Paper No. 6, July 2014.

Partnership for Peace Consortium of Defense Academies and Security Studies Institutes, "Defense Education Enhancement Program," web page, undated. As of November 2015:
http://www.pfp-consortium.org/index.php/activities/
defense-education-enhancement-program-deep

Paul, Christopher, Jessica Yeats, Colin P. Clarke, Miriam Matthews, and Lauren Skrabala, *Assessing and Evaluating Department of Defense Efforts to Inform, Influence, and Persuade: Handbook for Practitioners*, Santa Monica, Calif.: RAND Corporation, RR-809/2-OSD, 2015. As of October 27, 2015:
http://www.rand.org/pubs/research_reports/RR809z2.html

Perry, Walter L., Stuart E. Johnson, Stephanie Pezard, Gillian S. Oak, David Stebbins, and Chaoling Feng, *Defense Institution Building: An Assessment*, Santa Monica, Calif.: RAND Corporation, RR-1176-OSD, forthcoming.

Ploch, Lauren, *Africa Command: U.S. Strategic Interests and the Role of the U.S. Military in Africa*, Washington, D.C.: Congressional Research Service, RL34003, January 5, 2009, and July 22, 2011.

Polyakov, Leonid I., "Defense Institution Building in Ukraine," *Connections: The Quarterly Journal*, Vol. 7, No. 2, 2008, pp. 15–20.

Pritchett, Lant, Michael Woolcock, and Matt Andrews, *Capability Traps? The Mechanisms of Persistent Implementation Failure*, Washington, D.C.: Center for Global Development, Working Paper 234, December 2010.

Recalde, Marie, "Autorisant la ratification du traité instituant un partenariat en matière de coopération militaire entre la République française et la République du Sénégale [Authorizing the ratification of the treaty establishing a partnership in the field of military cooperation between the France Republic and the Republic of Senegal]," French National Assembly, Committee on National Defence and Armed Forces, Legislative Report No. 932, April 16, 2013. As of October 16, 2015:
http://www.assemblee-nationale.fr/14/rapports/r0932.asp

"Répartition des coopérants militaires," *Partenaires Sécurité Défense*, Vol. 274, June 2014, p. 6

Rice, Condoleezza, "U.S. Diplomatic Relations with Libya," statement by the U.S. Secretary of State, May 15, 2006. As of October 16, 2015:
http://malta.usembassy.gov/libya.html

Robathan, Andrew, parliamentary answer, House of Commons debate, September 17, 2011, col. 458W. As of October 16, 2015:
http://www.publications.parliament.uk/pa/cm201213/cmhansrd/cm120917/text/120917w0001.htm#120917w0001.htm_spnew26

Rodriguez, David M., "2014 AFRICOM Posture Statement," Statement Before the Senate Armed Services Committee, March 6, 2014.

Rosenlund, Stephen, "DIILS at 20 Years—Advancing the Rule of Law Worldwide," *JAG Magazine*, 2012, pp. 20–22.

Seib, Philip, and Carola Weil, "AFRICOM, the American Military and Public Diplomacy in Africa," USC Annenberg Policy Briefing, March 2008. As of October 14, 2015:
http://uscpublicdiplomacy.org/sites/uscpublicdiplomacy.org/files/legacy/pdfs/africom%20layout%20web.pdf

Simpson, Harold, *UK Sponsored Stabilisation and Reform in Sierra Leone 2002–2013: A Unique Case or a Template for Future Intervention(s)?* Royal Military Academy Sandhurst, Sandhurst Occasional Papers, No. 19, 2014.

Spencer, Claire, *The UK's Response to Extremism and Political Instability in North and West Africa*, London: Chatham House, Parliamentary Evidence, May 2013. As of October 16, 2015:
http://www.chathamhouse.org/sites/files/chathamhouse/public/Research/Middle%20East/0613pmnt_spencer.pdf

Tinti, Peter, "What Has the U.S. Already Tried in Mali?" *Christian Science Monitor*, November 20, 2012. As of October 16, 2015:
http://www.csmonitor.com/World/Africa/2012/1120/What-has-the-US-already-tried-in-Mali

Transparency International, *Global Corruption Barometer 2013*, 2013. As of October 16, 2015:
http://www.transparency.org/gcb2013/report

Transparency International UK, "Sub-Saharan Africa," Government Defence Anti-Corruption Index 2013, undated. As of July 2014: http://government.defenceindex.org

Under Secretary of Defense for Policy, *DoD Centers for Regional Security Studies*, Department of Defense Directive 5200.41, July 30, 2004 (certified current as of December 5, 2008). As of October 16, 2015: http://www.dtic.mil/whs/directives/corres/pdf/520041p.pdf

———, *Defense Institution Building (DIB)*, Draft Department of Defense Directive 5205.JB, Washington, D.C.: Department of Defense, as of May 11, 2015.

UNDP—*See* United Nations Development Programme.

United Nations Development Programme, *Human Development Report 2002: Deepening Democracy in a Fragmented World*, New York: Oxford University Press, 2002. As of May 15, 2015: http://hdr.undp.org/sites/default/files/reports/263/hdr_2002_en_complete.pdf

United Nations Mission in Liberia, "United Nations Documents on UNMIL," web page, undated. As of October 26, 2015: http://www.un.org/en/peacekeeping/missions/unmil/reports.shtml

United Nations Security Council, *Report of the Secretary-General to the Security Council on Liberia*, S/2003/875, September 11, 2003. As of October 16, 2015: https://unmil.unmissions.org/Portals/unmil/Documents/PDF/sg_reports/2003-sept-11.pdf

———, *Report of the Secretary-General on the United Nations Support Mission in Libya*, S/2014/653, September 5, 2014. As of January 2015: http://unsmil.unmissions.org/Portals/unsmil/Documents/Libya%20Report%20final%205%20Sept.%20%281%29.pdf

United Nations Support Mission in Libya, "Security Sector," web page, undated. As of October 16, 2015: http://unsmil.unmissions.org/Default.aspx?tabid=3556&language=en-US

———, *Towards a Defence White Paper*, April 2, 2013. Not available to the general public.

United States Institute of Peace, "Security Sector Governance," web page, undated. As of June 2014: http://www.usip.org/category/issue-areas/security-sector-governance

UNSMIL—*See* United Nations Support Mission in Libya.

U.S. Africa Command, *Liberia Country Cooperation Plan*, undated a. Not available to the general public.

———, "Operation Onward Liberty," web page, undated b. As of January 2015: www.africom.mil/what-we-do/operations/operation-onward-liberty

U.S. Africa Command Public Affairs, "AFRICOM Posture Statement: Ward Updates Congress on U.S. Africa Command," Annual Testimony to Congress, March 13, 2008. As of November 16, 2015:
http://www.africom.mil/newsroom/transcript/6136/africom-posture-statement-ward-updates-congress-on

——, "AFRICOM Posture Statement: Ward Reports Annual Testimony to Congress," Annual Testimony to Congress, March 9, 2010. As of November 16, 2015:
http://www.africom.mil/newsroom/article/7245/africom-posture-statement-ward-reports-annual-test

U.S. Agency for International Development, U.S. Department of Defense, and U.S. Department of State, *Security Sector Reform*, Washington, D.C., February 2009.

U.S. Department of the Army, *Stability Operations*, Field Manual 3-07, October 2008. As of May 15, 2015:
http://usacac.army.mil/cac2/repository/FM307/FM3-07.pdf

——, *Army Support to Security Cooperation*, Field Manual 3-22, January 2013a.

——, *Army Security Cooperation Handbook*, Washington, D.C., Pamphlet 11-31, March 5, 2013b. As of July 2014:
http://www.apd.army.mil/pdffiles/p11_31.pdf

U.S. Department of Defense, *Sustaining U.S. Global Leadership: Priorities for 21st Century Defense*, Washington, D.C., January 2012. As of October 16, 2015:
http://www.defense.gov/news/defense_strategic_guidance.pdf

——, *Quadrennial Defense Review 2014*, Washington, D.C., 2014. As of October 16, 2015:
http://archive.defense.gov/pubs/2014_Quadrennial_Defense_Review.pdf

U.S. Department of State, "Global Peace Operations Initiative (GPOI) 'Phase II' (Fiscal Years 2010–2014)," web page, undated a. As of July 2014:
http://www.state.gov/t/pm/ppa/gpoi/c47009.htm

——, "International Military Education and Training Account Summary," web page, undated b. As of August 2014:
http://www.state.gov/t/pm/ppa/sat/c14562.htm

——, "Peacekeeping Operations (PKO)," web page, undated c. As of July 2014:
http://www.state.gov/t/pm/65534.htm

Uzoechina, Okey, *Security Sector Reform and Governance Processes in West Africa: From Concepts to Reality*, Geneva Center for the Democratic Control of Armed Forces, Policy Paper No. 35, 2014.

Wall, Peter, and Allan Mallinson, *Defence Engagement: The British Army's Role in Building Security and Stability Overseas*, London: Chatham House, transcript, March 12, 2014. As of May 15, 2015:
http://www.chathamhouse.org/events/view/197403

Ward, William E., "United States Africa Command: 2009 Posture Statement," U.S. Africa Command Public Affairs Office, Annual Testimony to Congress, March 2009. As of November 16, 2015:
http://www.cfr.org/world/united-states-africa-command-2009-posture-statement/p20180

Watts, Stephen, *Identifying and Mitigating Risks in Security Sector Assistance for Africa's Fragile States*, Santa Monica, Calif.: RAND Corporation, RR-808-A, 2015. As of October 16, 2015:
http://www.rand.org/pubs/research_reports/RR808.html

Wehrey, Frederic, *Ending Libya's Civil War: Reconciling Politics, Rebuilding Security*, Carnegie Endowment for International Peace, September 2014.

Whitehouse, Bruce, "How U.S. Military Assistance Failed in Mali," *Bridges from Bamako* blog post, April 21, 2014. As of July 2014:
http://bridgesfrombamako.com/2014/04/21/how-us-military-assistance-failed/

The White House, "Political and Economic Reform in the Middle East and North Africa," Presidential Policy Directive 13, undated. Not available to the general public.

———, *National Security Strategy*, Washington, D.C., May 2010. As of October 16, 2015:
http://www.whitehouse.gov/sites/default/files/rss_viewer/national_security_strategy.pdf

———, *U.S. Strategy for Sub-Saharan Africa*, Presidential Policy Directive 16, June 2012. As of May 15, 2015:
http://www.state.gov/documents/organization/209377.pdf

———, "Fact Sheet: U. S. Security Sector Assistance Policy," Presidential Policy Directive 23, April 5, 2013. As of October 16, 2015:
https://www.whitehouse.gov/the-press-office/2013/04/05/fact-sheet-us-security-sector-assistance-policy

———, "Fact Sheet: Security Governance Initiative," web page, August 6, 2014. As of July 1, 2015:
https://www.whitehouse.gov/the-press-office/2014/08/06/fact-sheet-security-governance-initiative